D0962581

PRAISE FOR

TRANSFORMING CHILDREN INTO
SPIRITUAL CHAMPIONS

Remarkable! George Barna has done it again. America's expert number cruncher has analyzed the data and translated it into his most relevant work yet. Barna makes a compelling case that our hope for the future lies in our ability to help young people experience spiritual transformation. *Transforming Children into Spiritual Champions* will encourage and empower you to take a fresh look at our generational responsibility to grow our children into champions for the Lord.

TOMMY BARNETT
Senior Pastor, Phoenix First Assembly of God

The role of the church is to spiritually mentor parents; the role of parents is to spiritually mentor their children; and the legacy of faith continues from generation to generation. The theme of *Transforming Children into Spiritual Champions* is as old as the philosophy in the book of Deuteronomy and as fresh as today's newspaper. George Barna blends his incredible ability to research modern culture with his own passion to energize the spiritual life of children. It's a great book!

JIM BURNS
President and Executive Director, HomeWord Center for Youth and Family
at Azusa Pacific University

George Barna's book *Transforming Children into Spiritual Champions* is exactly what is needed today in youth ministry. More and more I find our staff wanting to know how to produce real life-long followers of Jesus. This book will be a great help! I'm particularly glad he addresses the evangelically sensitive topic of evaluation.

ROGER CROSS
President Emeritus, Youth For Christ/USA

Most people who trust Jesus as their Savior do so before the age of 15. Driven by this reality, George Barna invites us into the greatest harvest field of all time—children. In *Transforming Children into Spiritual Champions*, he boldly and faithfully calls on churches to seize the opportunity to impact their communities—starting with the children.

JACK D. EGGAR
President and CEO, Awana Clubs International

It is clear that the Lord is raising up a generation equipped with more knowledge, mobility, finances and communication than the world has ever seen. This generation occupies a unique place in history to be used by the Lord in amazing ways for His glory. The Church will miss this fantastic opportunity if we do not begin strategic ministry to children now. George Barna once again challenges the Body of Christ to take measurable action to equip this generation in *Transforming Children into Spiritual Champions*.

MARK MATLOCK
WisdomWorks Ministries

George Barna's point flies straight to the heart of every parent, teacher and pastor. Invest early. Get them while they're young, or they may miss knowing Jesus altogether—and thus, so may our world. *Transforming Children into Spiritual Champions* is a troubling read, requiring reconsideration of our priorities and focus in ministering to children—and their parents.

ELISA MORGAN
President Emerita, MOPS International

In *Transforming Children into Spiritual Champions*, George Barna reveals how we can be a vital part of the single most strategic ministry in God's kingdom, and in the process revolutionize life and faith in America. Without question, every pastor, leader and parent must read this book.

STEVE RUSSO
Evangelist and Author, *The Seduction of Our Children*
Co-host, "Real Answers"

Nothing has grabbed my attention more in the last two years than the Church's need to strategically focus our energies on children and youth. George Barna's *Transforming Children into Spiritual Champions* serves to underline this urgency for our local churches' allocation of time and resources.

MIKE SLAUGHTER

Lead Pastor, Ginghamsburg Church
Tipp City, Ohio

Few other communicators have the ability to paint as accurate a picture of the state of our children today as writer and researcher George Barna. By providing an assessment of both where we are and where we need to be in teaching and training the next generation, his book does indeed have the potential of transforming children into spiritual champions.

ED YOUNG

Senior Pastor, Fellowship Church
Dallas, Texas

TRANSFORMING CHILDREN INTO

SPIRITUAL CHAMPIONS

GEORGE BARNA

Regal

For more information and
special offers from Regal Books, email us at
subscribe@regalbooks.com

Published by Regal
From Gospel Light
Ventura, California, U.S.A.
www.regalbooks.com
Printed in the U.S.A.

First edition released by Regal in 2003.
Second edition released by Regal in 2013.

Library of Congress Cataloging-in-Publication Data
The Library of Congress has catalogued the first edition as follows:
Barna, George.
   Transforming children into spiritual champions / George Barna.
      p. cm.
Includes bibliographical references.
   ISBN 978-0-8307-3293-7 (hardcover), ISBN 978-0-8307-3294-4 (trade paper)
   1. Parenting—Religious aspects—Christianity.   2.   Spiritual
life—Christianity.   I.   Title.
   BV4529.B37 2003
   248.8'45—dc22
2003019313

Rights for publishing this book in other languages are contracted by Gospel Light Worldwide, the international nonprofit ministry of Gospel Light. Gospel Light Worldwide also provides publishing and technical assistance to international publishers dedicated to producing Sunday School and Vacation Bible School curricula and books in the languages of the world. For additional information, visit www.gospellightworldwide.org; write to Gospel Light Worldwide, P.O. Box 3875, Ventura, CA 93006; or send an e-mail to info@gospellightworldwide.org.

To order copies of this book and other Regal products in bulk quantities, please contact us at 1-800-446-7735.

CONTENTS

FOREWORD

Finally! I have been waiting almost 30 years for someone to put into book form what I have known to be true nearly all my ministry life: *Children matter!* They matter to God and to their parents, and they ought to matter more to the church.

With surgical precision, George Barna has cut through the veil of denial that most church leaders have lived in for far too long—the belief that we are doing enough in our churches to transform the average kid in our congregations into a spiritual champion. Painfully few churches have paid the price to break out of decades of status-quo ministry to children. Those that do break out soon discover a kind of anointing from God that suggests He might just favor churches that focus on and build up little ones.

We owe George a huge debt for writing this book.

Bill Hybels
Senior Pastor
Willow Creek Community Church

ACKNOWLEDGMENTS

Sincere thanks are due to the core research team at the Barna Research Group during the period while I was writing this book. The team—Lynn Gravel, Cameron Hubiak, Pam Jacob, David Kinnaman, Jill Kinnaman, Dan Parcon, Celeste Rivera and Kim Wilson—kept things running smoothly while I was focused on this project.

I am grateful to the dozens of pastors and church leaders who allowed us to conduct interviews, pore through church documents and poke around their ministry while we conducted the research for this book. I hope the time you invested will assist many other churches in becoming ministries that produce children who mature into spiritual champions.

I appreciate the patience and assistance of the team at Regal Books. In particular, thanks go to Kim Bangs, Deena Davis, Bill Denzel, Kyle Duncan, Bill Greig III, Bill Schultz and Rob Williams.

I am indebted to my family for letting me abandon them for a couple of weeks to put this book together. My wife, Nancy, and my daughters, Samantha and Corban, deserve a lot of credit for flexing with my intense schedule requirements. I pray that Nancy and I will be better able to raise our girls to be spiritual champions thanks to the insights we have gleaned from the research and the writing of this book.

Transforming Children Into

SPIRITUAL CHAMPIONS

I MISSED
THE OCEAN

Few people would have guessed that one day I'd become an impassioned advocate for ministry to children. Until recently, not even I would have bet money on that.

In my mind, children had always been part of a package deal: We want to reach adults with the gospel and then help them mature in their faith in Christ, so we have accepted the kids as a "throw-in." The paramount importance of serious, top-priority ministry to kids was not something I had ever taken too seriously.

My mind-set was not attributable to a lack of involvement in kids' lives. Over the years, I have had constant and satisfying interaction with young people: teaching in a public school, coaching basketball at a

Christian school, serving as a youth leader at a church, being an elder overseeing Christian education, studying the beliefs and behavior of young people through primary research, working as a board member for ministries focused on the needs of kids and being the father of two girls.

In fact, young people have always been on my radar screen. Ever the diligent researcher, I was capable of quoting the statistics related to the number of children in the United States, their quality of life, their behavioral and attitudinal patterns, how many have accepted Jesus Christ as their Savior, the nature of their spiritual beliefs and even their importance in drawing adults to churches. I knew a lot about kids and their plight in the local church, the schools, the marketplace and the home. I even wrote several books about teenagers, based on our nationwide studies.

Yet somehow the wisdom and necessity of seeing children as *the primary focus of ministry* never occurred to me. In that regard, perhaps I've simply been a product of my environment. Like most adults, I have been aware of children, fond of them and willing to invest some resources in them; but I have not really been fully devoted to their development. In my mind, they were people en route to significance—i.e., adulthood—but were not yet deserving of the choice resources.

Like many Christians, my life is committed to knowing, loving and serving God to the best of my ability. My focus has been to increase the spiritual health and cultural influence of the local church and the lives of individual believers. There is nothing I covet more than to someday hear the Lord say, "Well done, good and faithful servant." My assumption—never seriously challenged either by my own reflections or by the arguments of others—has been that the most efficient path toward receiving such an accolade from God would be through intense focus upon the moral development and spiritual transformation of adults.

I had never given alternative approaches serious consideration. After all, aren't *adults* the ones who call the shots in the world and determine the nature of our current and future reality? If the family is central to a healthy society and a strong Church, shouldn't we invest our resources predominantly in the *adults* who lead those units? When it comes to grasping the substance, the subtleties and the implications of the Christian faith, don't *adults* possess the greatest learning and intellectual capacities? Strategically, isn't it more important for us to equip *adults* so that they can use their gifts and resources to advance the Kingdom?

No, no, no and no. In retrospect, my view was so far off the mark that I didn't just miss the boat—I missed the entire ocean!

A TRANSFORMED MIND

Having spent the first two decades of my ministry engaged in research and leadership that targeted adults, the Lord has recently accomplished an extraordinary thing in my life. He changed my mind about the nature of effective ministry in our nation today.

For 20 years, credible and convincing information regarding the centrality of children to the health and future well-being of the Church was right in front of my eyes. During that time I'd consistently, although by no means exclusively, been working with ministries whose success could be traced to their wholehearted devotion to the needs and development of children. However, from the moment I'd accepted Christ at age 25, I'd been seduced into believing the great myth of modern ministry: Adults are where the Kingdom action is.

Somehow, God managed to lift the veil from my eyes long enough for me to gain wisdom. During the past couple of years, as I have been rethinking the foundations of church-based activity and seeking to understand how the Church might revolutionize life and faith in America, it became painfully clear to me that I had been operating on the basis of some very faulty assumptions.

Upon reprioritizing ministry to children, my perspective on ministry in its entirety has been revolutionized. My perceptions regarding worship, evangelism, discipleship, stewardship, community service and family—in short, just about everything related to ministry—have been altered. That is not to say that suddenly I know everything there is to know and you should therefore listen carefully and fall in line. Rather, this shift has enabled me to understand both situations that previously seemed too perplexing to comprehend and challenges too massive to voluntarily confront. Ministry will always be a difficult and sacrificial journey, but placing children in a more appropriate place in the landscape makes the journey more comprehensible and hopeful.

GOD'S METHOD

I have often heard Bible teachers claim that God meets you where you're at and leads you where you need to go, if you're willing to follow. I believe that is exactly what God has done in my life these past two years.

Almost every book I write is based on the same process: After considerable observation, discussion, prayer and reflection, I conduct primary research and analyze the results. Armed with the data, I seek confirmation of my interpretation through the real-world ministry experiences of churches and individuals. Confident that there is something valid to present, I then share the results through the written word.

It was through this standard practice that God opened my mind and heart to ranking ministry to children at the top of the priority list. He could have used any number of unusual tactics, but He chose to grab my attention not only in a way that made sense to me but also a way that would not allow me to deny the message. True to form, He contextualized the message for my consumption.

For this book, my company conducted a variety of nationwide surveys: a half-dozen surveys among adults and parents, a couple among teenagers and adolescents, four surveys among Protestant pastors and one project with church-based youth workers. After living with the data and placing it into a coherent perspective, we then conducted in-depth studies of the children's ministries in several dozen churches from across the nation to see if my hypotheses held true and to glean additional insights into effective ministry among kids. The contents of this book represent the tested and refined view from that two-year effort.

THE MISSION REVEALED

What does my epiphany have to do with you? I am not interested in simply informing you about the state of children and the opportunities to minister to them. Allow me to describe my prayer and goals for this book. My dream has five facets:

1. *Reach agreement.* If you do not share my view that ministry to children is the single most strategic ministry in God's kingdom, then I hope this book will challenge your prevailing notions. My thesis is that if you want your life to count for God's kingdom, there are many viable ways to use your gifts, talents and resources. However, if you want to have the greatest possible impact (i.e., to achieve a lasting legacy of spiritual dividends), then consider employing those resources in ministry to young people.

2. *See spiritual development as primary.* I have been discouraged to discover that most American adults—including most parents—see spiritual development of children as a value-added proposition rather than the single most-important aspect of children's development. You are invited to reconsider the priority of spiritual growth in the lives of children and to accept it as being more important than intellectual, physical and emotional development.

3. *Motivate to action.* It makes sense for us to reallocate the resources God has entrusted to us to those ministries and toward those people whom we can affect most positively for God's purposes. There is no group in greater need of such investment—or one that pays greater dividends on such investment—than children. Cognizant of the fact that most adults prefer to devote their ministry resources elsewhere, my desire is to challenge your current preference in favor of putting more into children's ministry.

4. *Facilitate the appropriate linkage.* In the course of reflecting on children and their spiritual growth, it is imperative that we understand God's expectations of how children should be nurtured. The local church is crucial in this process, but a child's family is central. Gaining a proper perspective on the

partnership between parents and church in the mutual effort to raise God-loving and God-fearing children is paramount. Enabling you to embrace that perspective and to support it is yet another objective of this book.

5. *See what it looks like.* Having studied many ministries, I want to describe the principles and models that we found to be common among the churches that effectively develop spiritually whole young people. I do not believe in prescribing a one-size-fits-all model for everyone to embrace; I have seen that approach undermine too many ministries. However, one of the processes that has served thousands of churches well in the past has been to identify common principles and best practices among effective churches. My hope is that those elements can be adapted to your ministry context without creating the need to accept and adopt an entirely foreign set of ministry philosophies, structures, values and programs.

Ultimately, the purpose of this endeavor is to enable the Church to engage in the process of transforming mere children into spiritual champions. It can be done. I know, because I have seen it firsthand, studied it closely and personally benefited from it. My earnest request is that you have an open mind long enough for me to make the case and then that you give this perspective your honest consideration. Let God lead you in your response—we may confidently trust that He knows how best to guide your life.

CHAPTER 1

THE STATE
OF AMERICAN
CHILDREN

They are more numerous than the entire Hispanic and African-American populations of the nation combined. They have more energy than a nuclear power plant and are as confounding as the federal budget. They have tastes as fluid as the Missouri River and dreams that will redefine the future. They are a marketer's pot of gold at the end of the rainbow and the most lovable and frustrating beings in the life of every parent.

We're talking about America's children. You don't have to look too hard to find them. In 2003, the Census Bureau reported that there were 73 million residents 18 years of age or younger living in the United States.[1]

They come in all shapes and various sizes, in many colors, and are distributed indiscriminately across the 50 states.

Our children will define the future, which makes them our most significant and enduring legacy. After all, God never told His followers to take over the world through force or intelligence. He simply told us to have children and then raise them to honor God in all they do. There-

Our children will define the future, which makes them our most significant and enduring legacy.

fore, you might logically conclude that bearing and raising children is not only our most enduring legacy but also one of our greatest personal responsibilities.

In this book, I will focus upon understanding and affecting the lives of children in the heart of the youth cohort (i.e., children in the 5- to 12-year-old age range).[2] This group, some 31 million strong, represents nearly half of the under-18-year-olds in the country. That's almost equal to the population of the entire state of California.

Why focus on this particular slice of the youth market? Because if you want to shape a person's life— whether you are most concerned about his or her moral, spiritual, physical, intellectual, emotional or economic development—it is during these crucial eight years that lifelong habits, values, beliefs and attitudes are formed.

FOUR DIMENSIONS OF OUR CHILDREN'S WELL-BEING

Everyone's life has challenges, difficulties and hardships en route to adulthood. On balance, though, most American children experience a good life, especially when compared to the quality of life children in many other nations of the world endure.

Educational Achievement and Intellectual Development

Most of America's children spend plenty of time in the classroom—and we pay for it. Public school systems throughout the nation spent more than $380 billion in 2000.[3] More children than ever before get an early educational start—more than half of all three- and four-year olds enroll in school, and nearly two-thirds of five-year-olds enroll in all-day kindergarten programs.[4] But neither school spending nor student attendance is a viable indicator of educational achievement or quality. Studies measuring such factors raise troubling questions.

For example, it is estimated that one-third of all school-aged children are at least one grade level behind in their academic performance.[5] Fewer than 3 out of 10 fourth graders read at grade level. Matters do not improve much over time. Just one-third of eighth graders are proficient in reading, and only one-quarter are proficient in writing and math.[6] These findings are particularly alarming given the correlation between poor academic skills and quality of life. Studies by the National Institutes of Health and the National Association for Educational Progress discovered that poor reading skills are a harbinger of teen pregnancy, criminal activity, poor academic achievement and dropping out before high school graduation.[7]

Testing among students reveals that when the academic performance of American pupils is compared to that of peers in other nations, American students come up far short. Recent studies of eighth graders in 25 industrialized nations showed that American students ranked tenth in science and twenty-first in mathematics.[8]

Interestingly, most parents are pleased with the quality of the schooling their young ones get. Gallup's recent research shows that 7 out of 10 parents are generally satisfied with the educational quality their children receive.[9] Our research found that most parents think their children are well cared for and well taught and have access to adequate facilities and programs. Relatively few parents believe their children are unsafe or exposed to unreasonable social pressures at school. Also interesting, most parents believe that the schools attended by most other children in the nation do not provide a quality education.[10]

Exposure to technology in the classroom is increasing in the United States. More than 4 out of 5 children under 13 years of age use a computer at school on a regular basis. Whether or not the integration of technology into the daily academic regimen will enhance students' learning experience remains to be seen.

Health and Physical Development

Advances in medical and health care have substantially reduced infant mortality during the past half-century. With new breakthroughs in medical research and technology, children have greater opportunities than ever before to live long and healthy lives.

There are, however, five dominant health-related challenges kids face these days. The most prevalent of these is being overweight. It is estimated that roughly 1 out of every 8 children under 13 is overweight or obese, which is double the figure of two decades ago. The combination of couch-potato behavior, computer games, fear of lack of safety in public places such as playgrounds and gymnasiums, supersized fast-food meals and the demise of school-run athletic programs contribute to the problem. While government agencies posit that only 25 percent of children ages two to five have a consistently healthy diet, that already low percentage shrinks to just 6 percent among teenagers.[11] Indeed, if lifestyle modeling is a significant influence on behavior, then the future looks even bleaker concerning the physical condition of our young people, since a variety of medical professionals have estimated that as many as 65 percent of adults are overweight or obese.[12]

Another serious concern is the increased sexual activity among youngsters. The Centers for Disease Control (CDC) report that almost 1 out of every 10 teenagers had sexual intercourse prior to his or her thirteenth birthday and that the number is steadily rising. Apart from the serious moral, emotional and spiritual consequences of premature sexual activity, such experiences commonly introduce sexually transmitted diseases (STD). CDC has reported that while relatively few adolescents have contracted an STD—fewer than 1 million of the youth under age 14—these young people are at greater risk than older individuals of acquiring one or more of the numerous permanent and incurable diseases, which is a particularly unnerving reality given the increasing sexual activity among children.[13]

Substance abuse—tobacco, drugs and alcohol—is a temptation to which millions of young people succumb. Current estimates indicate that about 1 out of every 10 eighth graders smokes daily (the proportion rises to 1 out of 4 by age 17); 1 out of 5 used drugs of some type in the past year (ranging from marijuana to hallucinogens to "club drugs" such as Ecstasy); and more than 1 out of 3 were drunk at least once in the past year, with significant numbers of adolescents reporting regular alcohol use and even binge drinking. For a small but significant percentage of those who abuse these substances, the behavior becomes addictive; and for a larger portion, the temporary impairment of their decision-making abilities produces serious physical consequences.

Being the victim of violence is yet another danger that threatens the health and well-being of millions of preteens. Forty-five percent of elementary schools reported one or more incidents of violent crime; the figure balloons to 74 percent, three-quarters, of all middle schools. In a typical year, 4 percent of elementary schools and 19 percent of middle schools report one or more serious violent crimes (e.g., murder, rape, suicide, use of a weapon or robbery). Students are subjected to violence most often in schools where gangs are present, and gangs are known to exist in nearly 3 out of 10 public schools. During a typical school year 1 out of every 14 students is threatened or injured at school with a weapon; 1 out of every 7 students is involved in a serious physical fight on school grounds. One common result, of course, is that millions of parents feel uneasy about their child's safety, and more than 1 million adolescents missed at least one day of school this past year due to fear of physical violence.[14]

More than 1 million adolescents missed at least one day of school this past year due to fear of physical violence.

Finally, the physical condition of young people is impacted by their medical care. Despite the attention focused on this issue in the past decade, 1 out of every 8 children under 13 has no health insurance and thus lacks adequate access to qualified medical attention. Combined with the skyrocketing cost of medical care, children suffer from medical challenges more widely than many people realize. One recent study noted that about 20 percent of youths in the United States exhibit some signs of psychiatric ailments and that most of those go undiagnosed.[15] One of the most widely discussed conditions is attention-deficit/hyperactivity disorder (ADHD), which afflicts about 7 percent of children in the 6- to 11-year-old age group. Millions of them are treated with Ritalin, antidepressants and other psychiatric drugs; millions more receive no treatment at all.

It should be pointed out that both the health of children and their engagement in at-risk behaviors have serious ramifications. A number of studies conducted in the past decade have demonstrated a strong correlation among six at-risk behaviors undertaken by adolescents—sexual intercourse, excessive drinking, smoking, use of illegal drugs, depression and suicide—and their generally negative impact.[16]

Economic State

During the past three decades, the economic state of children has actually improved. The federal government has expanded its support for children, currently funding more than 150 child-targeted programs to the tune of more than $50 billion annually.[17] While an unacceptably high proportion of young people (33 percent) will live in poverty before they reach adulthood, just half as many (17 percent) are mired in it at any given time.[18] (Realize that while the percentage is small, the human suffering is enormous—nearly 7 million American adolescents are plagued by poverty on any given day.) Most kids live in relatively suitable circumstances, and 8 out of 10 adolescents even report receiving spending money from their parents or extended family members. On average, adolescents are given an allowance of slightly more than $20 per week.

Emotional and Behavioral Development

Much of the emotional stability and maturity of children stems from their relationship with their family. Even though most parents feel they are doing a good job of raising their kids—and there is little doubt that most parents take their responsibility seriously—there is an abundance of evidence that suggests many overestimate their performance.

The effects of cohabitation, divorce, births to unmarried parents, and working mothers are taking a significant toll on a growing body of children—an impacted group that now numbers in the millions. One out of every 3 children born in the United States each year is born to an unmarried woman. One out of every 4 children presently lives with a single parent, and about half find themselves in that situation before they celebrate their eighteenth birthday. Three out of every 5 mothers of infants are in the labor force—roughly twice the proportion from just a quarter-century ago.[19]

The confluence of isolating factors has led a majority of parents of adolescents to admit that they do not spend enough meaningful time with their young ones.[20] Among kids 8 to 12 years old, one-third say they want to spend more time with their mother, in spite of the fact that today's preteens spend 31 hours per week with their mom, a jump of about six hours each week from two decades ago.[21] Adolescents spend less time with their fathers—an average of 23 hours weekly—which is also an increase compared to the early '80s. However, a substantial amount of the increases in parent-child time are attributable to an escalation in the amount of time spent driving to and from various activities, which is an endeavor not normally deemed a meaningful moment or quality time.

The good news is the slow rise in the percentage of kids who live with both biological parents (up from the 1 out of 2 a decade ago to nearly 6 out of 10 today). These families tend to be more financially and relationally stable, live in safer and more well-to-do areas and enroll their kids in higher-quality schools.

In spite of—or, maybe, thanks to—the changes in family realities, how are the kids turning out? There are many aspects to consider, but here are a few factors to ponder:

- Most adolescents consider themselves to be happy, loved, safe and optimistic about their future. However, we have found that most of them believe that adults generally consider young people to be rude, arrogant, lazy and sloppy.

- Kids ages 2 to 7 average nearly 25 hours per week of mass media intake; the figure balloons to almost 48 hours each week among those ages 8 to 13.[22] Evidence of the changing times and the new generation in place is the favorite medium of all, the Internet, according to 54 percent of kids under 8 and 73 percent of kids 8 to 12 years old.[23]

- Adolescents have become highly proficient at multitasking—the ability to juggle several activities simultaneously without losing ground in any of the areas.

- Young people admit to being highly influenced by their role models and to be actively seeking more such examples, but nearly half of all preteens (44 percent) admit that they don't have any role models.[24] While parents are the most commonly named role models, it is revealing that when children are asked to identify the three most important people in the world to them, only one-third name their mother or father. Even so, the vast majority of young kids—more than 9 out of 10—say they get along well with their parents, and most have no desire to have their parents eliminated from their lives.[25]

- A sign of the fears and pressures that weigh most heavily upon children is provided by the dominant social concerns named by adolescents: retaining and protecting their personal rights and freedoms, dealing with the presence of guns in their school, the prevalence of drunk driving, issues related to self-esteem, educational quality and drug abuse.[26]

- Kids stay busy. If it's not the crunch of homework, then it's the frenetic involvement in after-school and extracurricular activities. Even during the summer, two-thirds of all adolescents (64 percent) are booked into a full slate of activities.[27]

- The world is becoming more complex, but kids maintain the same basic needs as they have for decades: to be trusted, to be loved, to feel safe and to identify a significant purpose in life.[28]

THE MEANING BEHIND THE NUMBERS

If you have been working hard to stifle a yawn as I blazed through these figures and behavioral patterns, rest assured your reaction is quite normal. However, keep in mind that while numbers might not be your thing, the most important take-away from such a barrage of statistics is to determine the implications of the numbers. The value of research is that it allows you to form a portrait of reality, with each statistic representing another brushstroke in the picture. Armed with a clearer view of reality, you are prepared to respond more efficiently and meaningfully.

You don't need a series of surveys to remind you that life is messy. We prefer experiences and conditions to fit together into a simple, easy-to-interpret, black-and-white storyboard. But that is not often the case. More often, the emerging story is one riddled with inconsistencies, contradictions, rabbit trails and misleading irrelevancies. The narrative related to adolescents is no different. Adolescence is a season of life characterized by ups and downs, hopes and despair, victories and defeats, and constant changes. Finding the threads of truth that tie it all together is an art more than a science, and there are not many artists who can accurately and insightfully interpret the portrait.

Young people admit to being highly influenced by their role models but nearly half of all preteens admit that they don't have any role models.

What do the data regarding young people teach us? Many of the statistics that capture the public's attention tell the bad news. Yet if we examine all of the data, from various angles, we find that most kids face a few difficult challenges but generally live safe and satisfying lives. Each child has issues related to family, friends and lifestyle choices; but comparatively few kids are drug addicts, gang members, obese or dropouts. Most of our kids will not wind up as prostitutes or pimps in jail or number among the long-term unemployed.

The media headlines screaming "crisis" every other day are not designed to communicate truth but to capture market share and sell products. As consumers of information, we must retain some level of perspective. Granted, most of the nation's adolescents face serious threats and temptations, but most of them cope with those challenges fairly well. Yes, there are thousands of kids who live in despicable conditions or who consistently make awful choices—their situations are gut wrenching and deserve our best thinking and responses—but those kids are the anomalies, not the norm.

However, another spin on these statistics relates to the trajectory of the curves. While the behavioral and situational indicators may not suggest that the nation's children are engulfed in a large-scale, all-encompassing crisis, there are ample reasons to be concerned about the path of their development and the environment in which they are maturing.

Most of our young people will not end up as alcoholics or drug addicts, but most of them will abuse those substances on an irregular basis and will have one or more close friends who are serious substance abusers. Fortunately, most children will never be the victims of a serious physical crime, but most of them will experience daily fear and scheduling limitations as a result of the growing instances of juvenile violence. Fewer than 20 percent of kids will drop out of school before receiving a high school diploma, but the bigger danger may be their lack of desire to learn or their disinterest in personal excellence. Relatively few youngsters will be physically abandoned by their parents, but millions will be traumatized by receiving their parents' emotional leftovers, as well as by the divorce, separation or adulterous activities that will shatter their family unity. The majority of America's kids are not clamoring for X-rated, profane and violent content on TV or in movies and video games, but they are constantly seduced and tantalized by messages and imagery that blur or overstep the boundaries of decency. Maybe our young ones are not the sexually depraved beings that some have charged, but we must recognize that their perceptions of sexual propriety have been sufficiently compromised and that most kids will wind up with a sexually transmitted disease and an unfulfillable longing to return to virgin status.

Our nation's children will struggle to maintain a healthy balance in life. Constantly exposed to evil, they will win the battle most of the time but never escape the sense of jeopardy. They will seek to live a normal life but fall prey to the constantly deteriorating definitions of normality. The end result of growing up in this challenging culture will be a country of adults whose standards have been lowered and whose sensitivities have been blunted. The gifts of childhood that have become or are rapidly becoming extinct include innocence, civility, patience, joy and trust.

THE MISSING LINK

Many of the choices and outcomes in children's lives relate to two things that we have yet to examine: the moral and spiritual dimensions.

Often we seem bent on ensuring that the next generation will have a better life than did the preceding generations—the ability to live "the good life." But we define that life as the presence of comfort and security combined with the absence of hardship and disappointment. Well-intentioned parents often try to buy experiences and environments that foster a soft and satisfying lifestyle for their progeny.

In contrast, a biblical understanding of "the good life" is one that provides and exploits opportunities in order to experience, obey and serve God and other people. The existence of difficulties, failures and even persecution are not so much indicators of failure as they are events that build character and test our resolve to know, love and serve God. If life is primarily about our participation in a spiritual battle, then we must expect to encounter trials and pitfalls. The route to significance and success, therefore, demands that we develop the moral and spiritual foundations that permit us to lead holy and servantlike lifestyles.

Even though all of the above-noted statistics are current and accurate, they leave us with an incomplete picture of the lives of our nation's children. To round out that portrait we must study the moral and spiritual dimensions of the lives of young people. Let's take a deeper look at these matters.

CHAPTER 2

THE SPIRITUAL HEALTH OF OUR CHILDREN

The most significant aspect of every person's life is his or her spiritual health. Some people would argue that other dimensions are more important—the physical, intellectual, relational, professional, moral, socioeconomic and so forth. At the risk of being perceived as intolerant or politically incorrect, let me simply say that they are wrong. Every dimension of a person's experience hinges on his or her moral and spiritual condition. Let me illustrate the point.

Sociologists have found a strong correlation between socioeconomic standing and quality of life. That's not surprising, of course, since money is crucial to acquiring the basics that foster survival. However, people's reactions to their socioeconomic status are also closely tied to their faith. Many poor people experience greater levels of joy and fulfillment in life than do affluent individuals, because their view of life is based on the depth of their relationship with God rather than upon their personal achievements and comfort. Instead of defining success as the accumulation of possessions, experiencing the most exhilarating adventures or gaining public acclaim, many economically deprived people realize a greater degree of peace and joy because they view life as nothing more than a prelude to a more glorious existence with God in heaven. Their physical and emotional suffering is deemed secondary to the security they have in Christ's love. Their affluent peers who do not see God's hand at work in their lives will more likely lead comfortable but unsatisfying lives. The difference between these groups is their perception of the role of God and faith.

Viewed from another angle, consider the stories of individuals who have survived accidents but have been left with physical limitations.

How people view God and His role in their lives determines how they handle the cards dealt to them.

You will find that there are two types of reactions to such life-changing events: Some who emerge with disabilities see God at work, sparing them from a premature death while challenging them to enjoy and experience life in a new way. Others turn bitter over the loss of physical wholeness and criticize God for being absent in their time of need. As you might expect, the former group is typically composed of people who have a deep relationship with God while those who do not have such a relationship dominate the latter group. Again, how people view God and His role in their lives determines how they handle the cards dealt to them.

And so it is with children. We can strive to give our youngsters all the advantages the world has to offer, and motivate them to make the most of available opportunities and resources; but unless their spiritual life is prioritized and nurtured, they will miss out on much of the meaning, purpose and joy of life.

ARE ALL OF OUR DECISIONS SPIRITUALLY BASED?

An even deeper argument exists for the significance of a child's spiritual and moral development: Every choice we make is ultimately a spiritual decision. No matter what the issue or challenge is that we face, our decision comes down to what we believe is right or wrong, which is based squarely on our sense of truth and purpose. Our perspective on such matters comes from our spiritual beliefs, since our notions of meaning, purpose, truth, value, integrity, morality and ethics all stem from our ideas about the ultimate determinants of life.

Every choice we make is ultimately a spiritual decision.

As children mature, they are faced with numerous questions and choices regarding how to live. They take cues from their environment—particularly from the people they trust—as to how to respond to the dozens of choices they make every day. Unless children are shown the moral and spiritual implications of their choices, such factors are overlooked, often resulting in unfortunate or unforeseen consequences.

Many Americans believe it is an intellectual stretch to suggest that every choice we make is spiritual at its foundation. For instance, some might wonder how something as commonplace and seemingly unspiritual as the entrée they choose at dinner affects their spiritual lives. They fail to see that the content of the food ordered affects the health of their bodies, which in turn affects their ability to fulfill God's calling and purposes for their lives. Additionally, the entrée will cost them money. The expense of the meal affects the amount of money they will have to apply toward the priorities they have established in their lives, whether that entails spending in ways that maximize their personal comfort, donating funds to meet the needs of the poor or any of the thousands of other ways the money could be spent. In fact, the choice of whether to eat in a restaurant or at home, as well as the selection of which restaurant to patronize, is a reflection of their sense of responsibility to God, family, community and culture.

The Bible alerts us to the fact that someday we will have to give an account to God for every choice we made (see Eccles. 11:9; Rom 14:12).[1] This includes how we utilized every resource He entrusted to us on His behalf, which encompasses money, relationships, ideas, time, possessions and words. It follows, then, that the only viable defense we will muster for a specific choice relates to the moral and spiritual foundation of that decision, because that is the basis of God's judgment.

Friends sometimes tell me that such ruminations are overthinking or overspiritualizing life. Yet such thinking stems from one's worldview, which reveals one's foundational belief about the purpose and nature of life. For example, if you believe that life is about knowing, loving and serving God, then every decision, no matter how small and seemingly insignificant, must be run through a spiritual filter. In fact, even a cursory reading of Jesus' life on Earth shows that He was deliberate in His choices as to where to go, whom to associate with, what to say and how to evaluate situations. In short, everything He did was done for a reason, and His reasons always related back to His relationship with God the Father and His rules for living a holy life. The more you study the body of statements and behaviors pertaining to Jesus' brief public life as related in the New Testament, the more it becomes clear that every choice has consequences, and those consequences are ultimately about our relationship with God.

If your life is to be lived for a grand purpose—namely, to love God with all your heart, mind, strength and soul, and to love others as you love yourself—then you must evaluate each choice you make in light of its consistency with that purpose (see Luke 10:27). Most people fail to think about the connections made between their decisions and every other aspect of their lives, as well as to their bond with God. In other words, people rarely ponder the spiritual and moral implications of their choices. However, their refusal to reflect on the connections does not eliminate the connections or the spiritual consequences of their choices.[2]

Can I expect children to understand these matters? No, these matters are too complex and require too much knowledge of faith, truth, love and God's ways to emerge naturally within the context of a postmodern culture.[3] As respected pastor Jack Hayford has written, "No child naturally knows how to live in a manner that brings blessing to themselves and others."[4]

How, then, will children gain such an understanding? Part of my responsibility as a parent and as a member of the community of faith is to expose young children to the history, the expectations and the ways of God. During their formative years, children develop their decision-making perspectives and patterns. Helping them in that process is one of the most important responsibilities we have as humans; engaging them at a young age is a critical strategic choice. Jesus' teaching in the opening verses of Matthew 18 suggests that if we, as parents and counselors to the young, lose our interest in and sensitivity to children, we have shirked one of the most important duties given by God to humankind.

> PASTORAL
> **P** URGENT CONTENT
> ADVISORY
>
> **During their formative years, children develop their decision-making perspectives and patterns.**

In order for our children to grow into whole and healthy people, we must help them build strong foundations to prepare them for the rest of their lives. Because everything is ultimately a spiritual and moral issue, the more intentional and clear minded we are regarding their spiritual development, the better off they will be for the duration of their lives. We will discuss this more extensively in subsequent chapters.

DO OUR CHILDREN REALLY UNDERSTAND SPIRITUAL TRUTHS?

If we accept the notion that the moral and spiritual dimension of life is so crucial to the quality of life and spirit of children, we must ask how they are doing in this area. To gain perspective, I have conducted extensive research among randomly selected national samples of 13-year-olds. The surveys were administered to young people of that age because it is the best means we have of assessing what kids are absorbing during their adolescent years as they enter the next phase of their development cycle (i.e., the teen years).

In the remainder of this chapter, we will discuss what this research reveals about our children.

Jesus Christ as Personal Lord and Savior

Nine out of 10 young people (93 percent) consider themselves to be Christian by age 13. For a large portion of those kids, however, being Christian does not correspond to having a grace-based personal relationship with Jesus Christ; and for a large share of the self-professed Christians, commitment to that faith is minimal.

Among those who say they are Christian, only 35 percent indicate that they are "absolutely committed to the Christian faith." A majority, 54 percent, say they are "moderately committed," while the remaining 10 percent says they are not committed to Christianity.

A different way of assessing the faith commitment of young people is to determine whether they are evangelical, born again, nominal Christian, aligned with a non-Christian faith, or an atheist or agnostic. If born-again Christians are described as those who say they have made an important personal commitment to Jesus Christ and who believe they will have eternal life solely because they have confessed their sins and accepted Jesus Christ as their Savior, then we estimate that 34 percent of children are born again by age 13.[5]

A subset of the born-again segment are the evangelicals. These individuals are not only born again but also have a belief system that is more strongly aligned with biblical teachings in specific areas. Evangelicals would strongly affirm the accuracy of all biblical teachings, the personal responsibility to share their faith in Christ with nonbelievers, the centrality of faith in a person's life, the inability to attain eternal salvation except through the grace of God through Jesus Christ's death and resurrection, the nature of God as the creator and sustainer of all that exists, and the existence of Satan (God's enemy) as a real being, not merely a symbol of evil. Using this approach, just 4 percent of all 13-year-olds are classified as evangelicals.[6]

This leaves us with a majority of self-professed Christians as being neither evangelical nor born again. In total, 59 percent of all 13-year-olds are "notional Christians"—people who say they are Christian but are not committed followers of Christ in any discernible way.

Surprisingly, few young people have embraced other faith views by age 13. Only 3 percent are associated with a non-Christian faith (led by Judaism), and 4 percent claim to be either agnostic or atheist.

A series of studies we conducted regarding the age at which people accept Christ as their Savior highlights the importance of having people invite Jesus into their heart as their Savior when they are young. We discovered that the probability of someone embracing Jesus as his or her Savior was 32 percent for those between the ages of 5 and 12; 4 percent for those in the 13- to 18-age range; and 6 percent for people 19 or older. In other words, if people do not embrace Jesus Christ as their Savior before they reach their teenage years, the chance of their doing so at all is slim.

The importance of building strong spiritual foundations at an early age is again confirmed by recognizing that in 2003, there was virtually no difference between the spiritual standing of adults and those exiting their childhood years. Specifically, 4 percent of 13-year-olds were evangelicals compared to just 6 percent of adults; 34 percent of the 13-year-olds were born again, which was slightly less than the 38 percent found among adults. In other words, by the age of 13, your spiritual identity is largely set in place. Thousands of people decide to embrace Christ as their Savior each year, but from a statistical vantage point the number of Christians is not increasing—the new believers are essentially replacing the Christians who died or those who renounced their faith in Christ. My tracking of religious beliefs and behavior for more than a quarter century has revealed that the spiritual condition of adolescents and teenagers changes very little, if at all, as they age. When significant change is evident, it usually is attributable to a dramatic intrusion of the Holy Spirit into their lives.

Religious Involvement

Young people partake in a lot of religious activity during a typical week. Since most of them claim to be spiritual people and consider their faith to be very important in their lives, this level of religious involvement is not surprising.

Ninety-one percent of 13-year-olds pray to God during a typical week. Other common religious activities include attending church services (61 percent), attending a Sunday School class (52 percent) and donating some of their own money to a church (50 percent).

Fewer than half of all 13-year-olds engage in the following religious endeavors: attending a small group that meets away from the church grounds for some religious purpose (45 percent), reading from the Bible other than while at church (45 percent), attending a church-based youth activity other than Sunday School or a small group (44 percent) and reading from a sacred text or book other than the Bible (33 percent).

More than 4 out of 5 young people want to have a close relationship with God as a cornerstone in their lives.

Put it all together and there is one inescapable conclusion: Most adolescents are involved in religious activity of some type. Deeper analysis of that engagement, however, reveals that while many young people are intrigued by spirituality and seek a deeper understanding and experience, just as many are involved because one or more of the individuals in their relational circle—often known as their tribe—want to be involved in faith activities and thus bring the entire tribe along for the shared experience, which then deepens their relational connection. For the former group, faith is the driving motivation; for the latter group, faith is an excuse that facilitates the strengthening of their surrogate family.

Religious Beliefs

As is true among adults, most kids possess an odd palate of spiritual beliefs. Some biblical views are nearly universally held. For instance, 9 out of 10 young people accept the existence of God, the existence of the Trinity, the indwelling of the Holy Spirit in genuine disciples of Christ (92 percent) and the fact that every person has an eternal soul (91 percent). More than 4 out of 5 want to have a close relationship with God as a cornerstone in their lives.

Two-thirds or more of the nation's 13-year-olds are at least somewhat persuaded that the Bible is totally accurate in its teachings, that they have a personal responsibility to share their religious beliefs with others and that circumstances do not justify theft.

But there are many pieces of evidence exposing the theological confusion that plagues the minds of millions of young people.

Three-quarters believe the following:

- The devil does not exist—Satan is just a symbol of evil.
- A good person earns entry into heaven by doing enough good works.
- People are born morally neutral and make a choice as to become good or bad.
- All of the sacred books from different religious traditions (i.e., the Bible, the Koran, the Book of Mormon, and so forth) are merely different expressions of the same spiritual truths and principles.
- Spiritual and moral truth can only be discovered through logic, human reason and personal experience.

Two-thirds believe the following:

- Praying to deceased saints can have a positive effect on your life.
- The Bible discourages sin but never describes it as an innate behavior.

Half or more than half contend the following:

- Life either has no meaning or the meaning is realized through hard work, which produces the resources to enjoy comfort and security.
- There are no absolute standards for morals and ethics.
- Life is either a random series of acts or predetermined, but we have no real say in how our lives unfold.
- When Jesus Christ lived on Earth, He committed sins.
- The Bible does not specifically condemn homosexuality.

To place these views in context, realize that only 3 percent of the nation's 13-year-olds have a biblical worldview, which serves as the foundation for their decision making. This is partially because young people are more likely to base their decisions on their feelings (37 percent) or

TABLE 2.1

A COMPARISON OF RELIGIOUS BELIEFS OF 13-YEAR-OLDS AND ADULTS

Description of the belief statement	Strongly agree	Strongly disagree	Group
Your religious faith is very important in your life.	69%	5%	adults
	68	7	kids
The Bible is totally accurate in all of its teaching.	45	13	adults
	45	8	kids
You, personally, have a responsibility to tell other people your religious beliefs.	34	27	adults
	40	13	kids
The devil, or Satan, is not a living being but is a symbol of evil.	45	21	adults
	41	17	kids
If people are generally good, or do enough good things for others during their life, they will earn a place in heaven.	37	26	adults
	35	24	kids
When Jesus Christ lived on Earth, He committed sins.	25	37	adults
	22	42	kids
When people are born, they are neither good nor evil; they make a choice between the two as they mature.	58	15	adults
	63	6	kids
God is one Being in three separate and equal persons— God the Father, Jesus Christ the Son and the Holy Spirit.	70	9	adults
	61	11	kids
Every person has a soul that will live forever, either in God's presence or absence.	64	8	adults
	62	5	kids
A human being can be under the control or the influence of spiritual forces such as demons.	31	25	adults
	34	24	kids

Source: National surveys conducted by Barna Research Group in 2001-2003. Sample sizes range from 630 to 1,010 adults and 126 to 318 13-year-olds.

upon what other people expect of them (26 percent) rather than depend upon the Bible as their standard for moral choices (8 percent). But it also is partly attributable to the theological distortions that young people embrace as truth.

The chances of seeing the worldviews of young people change to be more reflective of biblical truth are slim. We know this based upon two convincing bits of evidence. First, a large majority of young people believe that they know every major story and principle on which the Christian faith is based, and thus they feel secure in their understanding of Christianity. Consequently, more than 2 out of every 3 13-year-olds argue that they will not alter any of their core beliefs in the future. In other words, they are closed to learning new biblical insights or correction regarding erroneous perspectives.

Second, we find an astounding level of consistency between the religious beliefs of adults and children. This has two implications. Initially, it suggests that whatever beliefs a person embraces when he or she is young are not likely to change as the individual ages. (This is a variation on the "first impressions die hard" theory.) In addition, the consistency means that the average young person will encounter fewer adults or peers whose worldview is sufficiently different enough as to pose a serious challenge to his or her own existing belief system.

WHAT DOES THE CHURCH HAVE TO DO WITH IT?

Churches, of course, have a vested interest in the spiritual condition of children. However, an assessment of the importance that churches attach to ministering to children can be confusing.

A compelling sign of the significance assigned to children is the existence of a full-blown children's ministry in virtually every church in the nation, complete with designated facilities and equipment, the purchase of Sunday School curriculum and educational resources, a full complement of teachers assigned to instruct kids each week, special programs administered during the year (e.g., Vacation Bible School, Mothers of Preschoolers, concerts, field trips and summer camps) and a series of safety procedures carried out to protect children from harm. Other signs include one or two sermons regarding the importance of children being preached during a typical ministry year, and having the entire congregation occasionally pray for the spiritual health and development of the church's young people.

Yet some signs indicate that children are not a high ministry priority. Among these are the fact that most church leaders we interviewed—pastors, staff and elders—are uninformed as to the spiritual content and practices related to their children's ministry, and almost none of those church leaders is able to provide specific insights into how satisfactorily the children are maturing in their faith. (Attendance figures and the publisher of the curriculum purchased are widely known among church leaders, but those same leaders are rarely able to quote specific measures of children's spiritual growth.)

This sense of limited priority is confirmed by research we conducted among a random national sample of senior pastors leading Protestant churches. When asked to identify their church's top ministry priorities for the current year, only 24 percent mentioned ministry to children.

The attention devoted to the children's ministry most frequently revolves around making sure there are teachers in place, rooms available and a standardized curriculum ready to be used. I also have discovered that most churches are interested in acquiring a turnkey curriculum—resources that require minimal administration by the church, minimal preparation time by the teacher, minimal prior knowledge by the students and the provision of all the ideas, materials and directions needed to fill the entire class time.

These issues are not solely related to church leadership. More than two-thirds of all Protestant churches admit that they struggle to recruit and retain adults who will serve as instructors and helpers in the classroom. Parents are the natural choice, but they are typically eager to drop off their kids so that they can enjoy some time for their own spiritual nourishment and a break from their kids. The adults who agree to serve in the classroom are often minimally qualified and barely trained for their duties. While they deserve sincere gratitude and admiration for willingly participating, many of them are ill equipped to leave a lasting and positive spiritual imprint on the children entrusted to them. Two of their often-heard complaints are that they do not believe they have been given the authority to institute the level of discipline sometimes called for and they are not able to demand the depth of commitment that children and their parents need to make in order to see significant life change occur. Without that mantle of authority, many of these volunteers lament that they feel as if they are engaging in church-sanctioned babysitting rather than spiritual transformation.

Perhaps nothing makes the relative unimportance of children's ministry clearer than budget realities. In the average Protestant church, approximately 41 percent of the people who attend the church on a typical weekend are under the age of 18—and that figure jumps to nearly 50 percent if we include all of the young people involved in some type of church-based, faith-related activity on the church campus throughout the entire week. Yet, less than 15 percent of the average church's ministry budget is allocated to the needs of the children's ministry. (Precise figures are very difficult to develop since churches track their spending differently, and it is hard to allocate some facility and personnel costs appropriately.) Regardless of the exact figures, the pattern is evident: Children receive a relatively minor share of the church's ministry dollars. If the popular adage that one's checkbook identifies one's priorities is correct, then children are clearly a secondary concern for most churches.

Furthermore, the second-class status of nurturing children is evident upon exploring how churches staff their ministry. In the small proportion of churches that have ministry personnel beyond the senior pastor (Almost 20 percent of Protestant congregations have ministry staff other than support personnel such as secretaries and administrative assistants), hiring someone to direct children's ministries is often seen as a luxury rather than a necessity. Assistant pastors, worship leaders and pastors to teens (i.e., youth pastors) are usually considered to be higher priorities than are individuals who focus primarily upon the needs of children. In most cases, other personnel such as office assistants, maintenance workers and professional subcontractors (e.g., lawyers and accountants) also are brought onto the payroll long before a director of children's ministries is invited aboard.

One of the more disturbing findings from my research has been that church leaders often view the children's ministry as a "loss leader"—a retail term used to describe the marketing of a product that loses money but generates a sufficient payback through ancillary benefits. Children's ministries are frequently marketed to adults because research shows that millions of parents want their children to have a positive church experience and that they will attend any nearby church that provides their children with a consistently high-quality ministry. Viewed from that angle, many churches do not adequately or appropriately support ministry to children because kids are seen as the "bait" that enables the church to land the real treasure—i.e., adults—rather than as a valuable, if unrefined, treasure in themselves.

ARE WE MISSING THE MARK?

The statistics pertaining to the spiritual life and experience of children are rather alarming. Given the trends indicating that your spiritual condition by the age of 13 is a strong predictor of your spiritual profile as an adult, it seems clear that a deep and robust spiritual life demands intentional and strategic spiritual nurturing during the early childhood and adolescent years.

We spend roughly 68 times more money per capita on caring for the average felon than on a church's ministry to a spiritually hungry child.

Consider the facts. People are much more likely to accept Christ as their Savior when they are young. Absorption of biblical information and principles typically peaks during the preteen years. Attitudes about the viability and value of church participation form early in life. Habits related to the practice of one's faith develop when one is young and change surprisingly little over time.

Although we spend roughly 68 times more money per capita on caring for the average felon than on a church's ministry to a spiritually hungry child and we spend substantially more on church buildings and maintenance than on raising up spiritual champions among our progeny, I don't believe the central issue is finances. More than anything, it is an issue of understanding the incredible importance of developing strong, spiritual foundations early and reinforcing those foundations as the child ages.

With widespread accessibility to the Internet, millions of Americans have jumped into investing in stocks, bonds and other financial instruments. The hope of amateur investors is to strike it rich by achieving a great return on investment. Yet if we could see the world through God's eyes, we would quickly recognize that the only return on investment that truly matters is lives transformed to love God more deeply and to obey Him more perfectly. As you ponder how to invest your personal resources of all types—time, money, experience, ability, facilities, expertise and so on—keep in mind that there is no better investment than nurturing our youngsters for an eternal payback.

The research reinforces one simple but profound truth over and over again: If you want to have a lasting influence upon the world, you must invest in people's lives; and if you want to maximize that investment, then you must invest in those people while they are young. The research simply crystallizes lessons that we can observe through history and personal experience. In other words, if you connect with children today, effectively teaching them biblical principles and foundations from the start, then you will see the fruit of that effort blossom for decades to come. The more diligent we are in these efforts, the more prodigious a harvest we will reap. Alternatively, the more lackadaisical we choose to be in our efforts to raise up children as moral and spiritual champions, the less healthy the Church and society of the future will be.

The choice is yours.

CHAPTER 3

WHY KIDS MATTER

Some years ago I was driving through the central business district of Trenton, New Jersey. As the fellow driving the vehicle slowed to a stop at a red light, we watched a group of a half-dozen elderly men sitting on the front stoop of a red-brick row house, lazily consuming bottles of liquor under the scorching midday sun.

Calling attention to the assembly, I remarked on the sadness of the event and ended my thought by wondering aloud how God must feel watching these tired individuals waste away the final years of their lives. My car mate grunted with disdain, "God wouldn't give a hoot about those old geezers. They're not goin' anywhere. They don't matter."

The boldness of such a blatant dismissal of human life shocked me then, just as the commonplace rejection of children as significant recipients of ministry shocks me today. All people matter to God, regardless of their age, gender, ethnicity or nationality. And children seem to have a particularly tender place in His heart.

CHILDREN MATTER TO GOD

The Bible makes it quite clear that children are uniquely special to God. If you examine what the Scriptures say about children, you will discover how precious they are to Him. In His eyes, they represent a multitude of attributes and possibilities:

- *Children are a gift from God.* He grants children to adults as a special sign of His love to us and as a means of personal fulfillment (see Deut. 7:13; Ps. 127:3).

- *Adults receive special blessings through their children.* God provides supernatural benefits of many types to family and friends through children, and He matures us through the challenges of parenting (see Num. 5:28; Deut. 28:4,11; Lam. 4:2).

- *Children are desirable.* From the beginning of human history, God has instructed us to have children. In fact, the intentional decision of a married couple not to have children is viewed as a bad choice (see Gen. 9:7; Deut. 6:3; Luke 1:24-25).

- *Children need to be taught how to think and act in relation to God and His ways.* One of the greatest adult challenges is passing on appropriate knowledge and behaviors to their progeny. We were created to be in relationship with Him, so our understanding of His nature and expectations is a significant undertaking (see Exod. 12:26,37; Deut. 4:9-10; 6:1-7; 31:12-13; Ps. 78:4-6; Prov. 22:6).

- *To have a fruitful relationship with God, children must be taught to obey Him.* Obedience is one of the central duties of humankind. Throughout Scripture, God exhorts His people to be raised to follow His commands and reap the benefits of such obedience (see Prov. 8:32; 19:26; Jer. 2:30; 3:22; Eph. 6:1; Col. 3:20).

- *Children are so valuable to God that He commands us to protect them.* Parents are supposed to ensure the spiritual and physical security of their children (see 1 Sam. 20:42; Ezra 8:21).

- *God wants to have a genuine relationship with His children.* Accordingly, He describes how children may enter His presence and enjoy His company (see Pss. 8:2; 34:11; 103:13; Mal. 2:15; Matt. 21:15; Mark 10:13-16).

- *God loves children enough to ensure that they receive discipline.* Regardless of the manner in which that shaping is provided, it is a reflection of His passion for a child's well-being (see Prov. 3:11-12; 13:24; 19:18; 23:13; 29:15-17; Eph. 6:4).

- *God enjoys the nature and personality of children.* The Scriptures specifically identify attributes such as sincerity, humility, naivete, vulnerability and simplicity as qualities found in children, and He treasures these characteristics (see Matt. 18:3; 19:14; Phil. 2:15).

These perspectives from God concerning the importance of children provide a clear and undeniable message to us: If children matter this much to God, then they should matter as much to us, too.

The survey data described earlier (see chapter 2) give us further reason to make first-class ministry to children a top priority. One of the data trails pointed out that most people decide what they will do about Jesus—either wholeheartedly follow, merely acknowledge, or ignore or reject Him—while they are young. Most children are bombarded with cues regarding their eternal condition and fate, and they develop a rather deeply held perspective on the matter prior to entering high school.

Clearly, people who maintain that evangelizing and discipling children is a waste of time—that is, such efforts are better reserved for older individuals, when such an investment can reap a return—are arguing from a base of human reasoning, not from a foundation of hard, cold facts. While we must acknowledge that neither age nor any other barriers preclude God's sovereignty—there are millions of cases in which people connect with Him in their teenage or adult years—the truth is that such cases are not typical. More often than not, what a person decides about truth, sin, forgiveness and eternal consequences during the pre-teen years is the same perspective that person carries to the grave and beyond, wherever that may take him or her.

This is not simply an issue of effective evangelism, since genuine evangelism cannot be separated from authentic discipleship. God does not just want people to be saved from eternal damnation; He wants them to be transformed in every dimension of their earthly existence by the miracle of His grace. Children matter to God because He loves them and wants them to experience the best, right from the start of their lives. He relies upon us, their teachers and protectors, to deliver the guidance and experiences they need to grow in their understanding of love for and obedience to Him.

CHILDREN MATTER TO YOU AND ME

Take a moment to name the people who are leaders in your world today—those who influence your life through their role in government, business, community organizations, the Church and the media. Now

Can we afford to let the moral and spiritual dimension of our future leaders be shaped by default?

consider this: Each one of those individuals was once a child whose potential was identified, shaped and released by those who preceded them as leaders, teachers and other agents of influence. They were equipped to affect the world by those who saw promise in them and who were willing to sacrifice personal resources to advance that potential.

Now think about the children who will emerge as the future leaders of our world: government officials, community activists, clergy and parachurch professionals, business executives, school administrators and media directors. They may receive the basic education and training required to become effective leaders: reading, writing, mathematics, analytical thinking, relational skills, financial acumen, historical perspectives, and so forth. However, who will promote within them the single most-important set of skills they will need to succeed according to God's standards—their moral and spiritual bearings? Can we afford to let the moral and spiritual dimension of our future leaders be shaped by default?

Christians have a tremendous opportunity to help build a better, more God-honoring world by investing in the moral and spiritual character of future leaders. These trailblazers will need a full arsenal of tools to lead people to productive, meaningful, holy lives. Their most important tools—and the ones they will use most often—will be the moral and spiritual principles and practices they embody, which facilitate appropriate choices and enable them to model responsible behavior.

Age

Research regarding all facets of moral and spiritual development—whether related to worldview, beliefs or behavior—shows that such development starts as early as age two. The process then progresses rather quickly. Social scientists have known for years that the moral foundations of children are generally determined by the time the individual reaches age nine. Our research confirms a parallel outcome in the spiritual dimension: By age nine, most children have their spiritual moorings in place.

The implication of these findings is clear: Anyone who wishes to have significant influence on the development of a person's moral and spiritual foundations had better exert that influence while the person is still open-minded and impressionable—in other words, while the person is still young. By waiting until a person is in his or her late adolescent or teenage years, the nature of influential attempts must be significantly different, because the spiritual foundation has already been formed and integrated into the person's life. At that stage, spiritual influence requires a more complex process to dislodge what already exists prior to replacing it with a divergent perspective. Research data and personal experience inform us that it is far easier to have influence before the foundations are firm. The older a person gets, the more difficult it is for him or her to replace existing moral and spiritual pillars.

Our efforts to teach and nurture children are an investment in the future—theirs and ours. Children who are exposed to and embrace godly lives enjoy the lifelong benefit of God's blessings and significant opportunities for influential service. Adults who invest in those children will also reap a rich dividend as God's kingdom prospers through the efforts of those young people when they apply what they have learned for decades to come.

Ministry

I have been astonished to see how many church people resist a wholesale commitment to providing the best possible ministry to children. Most churches and faith communities pour the bulk of their resources into trying to affect the lives of adults and are often disappointed to find the return on investment minimal, at best.

Nearly half of the adults who attended church regularly as children and now bring their own offspring to a church do not even know Jesus Christ as their personal Lord and Savior, even after more than a quarter century of consistent church exposure and involvement!

The reason for the low yield is simple. First, the fundamental thought patterns, beliefs and behavioral patterns of adults were formed many years ago and are generally too entrenched to change without a radical commitment to personal transformation. Such a commitment comes at great cost and demands substantial focus. Most adults are simply not willing to go that route.

Second, because most adults received "ministry leftovers" (i.e., limited funding, minimal instructional resources and teaching that was ill-focused) when they were young, they became exactly what we made them: well-intentioned, inadequately nurtured, minimally equipped secular people who dabble in religious thought and activity. Nearly half of the adults who attended church regularly as children and now bring their own offspring to a church do not even know Jesus Christ as their personal Lord and Savior, even after more than a quarter century of consistent church exposure and involvement!

What we create in a young person's life determines that person's behavior as an adult. God can intrude in the process and change things dramatically, but parents and teachers are among the primary instruments of change through whom He works to bring about such transformation. You simply cannot raise a child to be a compliant workhorse and then expect him or her to turnaround and become a majestic thoroughbred when he or she is older.

Church

Many of us are deeply interested in seeing the Christian Church in America become a healthier expression of God's kingdom. But to see greater health emerge, we must pour a larger percentage of our vast resources into people rather than programs and buildings. The Church is, after all, nothing more or less than the accumulation of the people who know, love and serve Jesus. Buildings and programs serve a viable purpose, but the ultimate focus of our ministry endeavors must be about knowing, loving and serving people so that they become mature, committed followers and reflections of Jesus.

One kid leading another kid to the foot of the Cross for a life-changing encounter with Jesus is one of the most prolific and effective means of evangelism in the nation.

Having devoted more than two decades of my life and all of my professional skills to studying and working with ministries of all types, I am now convinced that the greatest hope for the local church lies in raising godly children. Think about the tremendous influence these unassuming little people possess: Every year, tens of thousands of parents are brought to faith in Christ because one of their children was so changed by his or her own relationship with the Lord that the parent could not ignore the power of Christ any longer. Further, we have discovered that peer evangelism among young children—one kid leading another kid to the foot of the Cross for a life-changing encounter with Jesus—is one of the most prolific and effective means of evangelism in the nation.

In addition, every year hundreds of thousands of unchurched people explore Christian churches in their search for a spiritual anchor. Among those who have children in tow, the largest share who get involved in congregational life select their church because of the quality of the children's ministry.

Children Matter on the Battlefront

Simply put, if you want to win a war, you must control the battlefront. In the complexity of the world these days, we sometimes lose sight of the fact that life is ultimately a spiritual battle and that each of us is a spiritual being who must declare a side in the war and then fight to the end for what we believe is truth. In that process, we must identify the boundaries of the battlefront before we can take command of it.

Where is the battlefront today? Is it to be found in the fight for the rights of the unborn or the call to outlaw homosexual behavior? Does it lie within the struggle to get adults to spend more than two hours per week at church or the hope of getting people to read the Bible every day? Will it be found at the heart of the culture wars, which pit biblical morality against the garbage imbedded in a lot of the movies, television and music to which we are exposed? Is the line in the sand drawn to separate those who selfishly work to accumulate resources for personal pleasure from those who seek to distribute resources more equitably?

No, I believe the battlefront is found in the minds, hearts and souls of our children.

Imagine yourself as Satan—an ugly and horrifying thought, for sure, but invaluable to make this crucial point—and remember that as the prince of darkness your driving motivation is to destroy God. You realize that His greatest weakness is that He loves people and that this love makes Him vulnerable to attack. You can hurt Him by hurting those whom He loves. What better way to get to God than through His beloved human creatures? And what easier way to inflict the maximum possible pain upon God than by winning over His beloved creatures from the earliest possible moment, resulting in a lifetime of unrighteous behavior by those creatures? Win them early, and the job is all but finished.

Now, return to your true persona. You are a lover and servant of God and therefore an enemy of Satan. Given Satan's single-minded purpose—destroy God and rule the universe—we can count on him to put his most destructive resources into play at the front lines of the eternal battle against God. Where are those front lines? In the minds, hearts and souls of children. Ever the strategic mastermind, Satan knows well that if you destroy the character and hope of children, you rule the world! Satan is not omnipotent, but he is intelligent and clever—certainly sharp enough to realize that if you win over children, you have won the war for at least one generation and probably more.

If we do a great job of training children to love God with all their heart, mind, strength and soul, then we will no longer have to invest time battling over moral and spiritual issues such as abortion, homosexuality, gambling and pornography. The ways of God will flow naturally from the lives of the people who have embraced Him and His principles. We could trust our children to do what is right, because entrenched in their heart, mind and soul is an unshakable understanding of what is right and a compelling desire to act accordingly.

The war will not be won by writing letters to the FCC, boycotting media corporations and advertisers or spending billions in the courtroom attempting to legislate morality. Those tactics are not bad, but they fail to address the root of the problem: people's alienation from God. If we effectively teach God's principles and expectations to our youngsters and instill within them a thirst for righteousness and a passion for God, the need to wage a culture war will be eliminated by reshaping the culture from within. The cumulative effect of their character and beliefs will redefine the contours of our culture.

Will we need to worry about how to motivate people to read the Bible, how to encourage people to attend worship services, how to raise enough money to maintain the ministry and how to get believers to pursue the Great Commission? Not if we help them early on develop a biblical worldview and unite them with a community of believers who will foster their commitment to God's truth and establish personal accountability for a faith-driven existence. Ultimately, the pervasive health of the Church will positively impact every dimension of society.

CHAPTER 4

WHAT KIDS NEED

As a young adult, prior to accepting Christ as my Savior and long before my wife and I had children, I embraced many unexamined assumptions about what children need to lead meaningful lives. My naïveté led me to conclude that if parents loved their kids and took care of their material needs, if the school did a good job of addressing intellectual growth, if the Church provided a regular diet of religious teaching and experiences and if the children had opportunities to engage in physical activities that facilitated both fun and fitness, then their lives would be robust, satisfying and meaningful.

Two decades later, armed with many research studies and numerous personal experiences with a variety of children and families, and tuned into a biblical worldview that places these matters in an entirely different light, I understand where many of my ideas about children's needs came from, how they were consistently reinforced by the perceptions and values widely embraced in American society, and how terribly wrong and even harmful such a perspective is.

SPIRITUALITY

The one thing I correctly understood is that human development is a complex mixture of growth in five core areas: the moral, spiritual, physical, emotional and intellectual dimensions of life. What I did not recognize is that the basis of each of these areas is one's spiritual foundation.

Think about how we grow in each of these areas. Morality, for instance, is all about determining and acting upon what we believe to be right or wrong. To distinguish right from wrong, we need to establish whether morals are absolute or situational—that is, whether they are always the same, regardless of the situation, or whether they are determined according to the circumstances. In order to arrive at that point of decision, we must identify the source of our moral standards. Most Americans contend that morals are relative because they are based upon a person's feelings, experiences, personal philosophy or personal needs. Relatively few American adults—barely 25 percent, and the percentage is consistently declining—say that there is an absolute moral standard and that it is contained within the Bible. As you can imagine, your decision as to the origin of moral truth and its nature brings with it significant consequences. The bottom line is that a person's moral foundation is either based upon Christian spirituality and thus drawn from God's Word, or it is based on worldly perspectives (i.e., pagan spirituality).

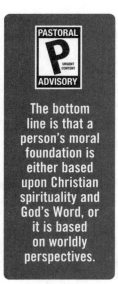

PASTORAL
P URGENT CONTENT
ADVISORY

The bottom line is that a person's moral foundation is either based upon Christian spirituality and God's Word, or it is based on worldly perspectives.

Your perspective on your physical condition and responsibilities also is based upon your spiritual perspective. Your notions of who gave you your body, why it is important and the ultimate purposes intended for your body affect how you treat and think about your body. A biblical point of view would be that it is designed to be an instrument óf blessing to God and others. If your ultimate reason for existence is to love God and other people, then your body is one of the tools provided to fulfill that responsibility. The more you take care of your body— without its becoming an obsession or an idol—the more capable you will be of fulfilling your purpose. If, however, you view your body from a worldly perspective (i.e., it is nothing more than a private asset that allows you to experience maximum enjoyment and pleasure in life), then you will not only miss out on true fulfillment, but you also are more likely to suffer from the physical disadvantages of a wayward view (e.g., sexually transmitted diseases).

Your emotional state can be analyzed in a similar manner. Your self-image and your feelings can be seen as a means of experiencing and enjoying the presence of God and receiving love and acceptance from Him, or you can seek to have your emotional needs met primarily by people and experiences. Because you were created by God to love Him and be loved by Him, and because He always provides perfect love, when you base your self-image and emotional wholeness on an appropriate and deepening relationship with Him, you will be satiated and satisfied. Alternatively, if you seek fulfillment through sensuality, popularity or even insularity, you will be profoundly disappointed. Seeking emotional wholeness through the means of the world rather than via spiritual means produces stress, depression, dissatisfaction and the like.

Even your intellectual fulfillment is meant to come through a spiritual conduit. How many millions of people live toward the goal of being the smartest in their field? Again, a biblical perspective keeps you grounded in this regard, as Solomon in the book of Ecclesiastes found that such striving for intellectual superiority or completeness is mere arrogance. There is nothing wrong with seeking empirical insight and pushing the boundaries of knowledge, of course, as long as the ultimate end is to love and serve God and His people more purely. The pursuit of knowledge for the sake of personal gain or reputation is vain and foolish.

A different slant on personal development is the emphasis upon character development. Naturally, you want your children to exhibit good character, demonstrating traits such as respect, courage, honesty, compassion, kindness, humility, generosity, gentleness, loyalty and the like. The values and morals that contribute to good character, however, come from a strong spiritual base. Without that base as a point of motivation, developing such attributes is less compelling.

The most important dimension of our lives, therefore, is the spiritual dimension. Sadly, millions of Americans have accepted the centrality of spiritual development but pursue spirituality apart from God's plan. Millions of American adults—more than 30 million, according to our research—align themselves with systems of faith and forms of spirituality that are inconsistent with biblical teaching. People are involved in hundreds of diverse religious sects and cults that have little or nothing to do with the ways and laws of God. Their moral, physical, emotional and intellectual perspectives and behaviors intersect with those that honor God only when such choices appear to be to their immediate and personal advantage.

Unfortunately, even most individuals who think of themselves as Christian do not truly operate on the basis of God's principles and expectations, except when it is convenient or inescapable. Again, our national research suggests that shockingly few Christian adults make their moral, physical, emotional and intellectual choices on the basis of sound reasoning from Scripture. The result is that they miss God's richest blessings and begin to question why God doesn't love them and doesn't take better care of them, and they even question if He is real.

Is that how you want your children to grow up—being in tune with God only when it seems to serve their best interests and losing out on the great life He has in mind for them if they would only pay attention and get with the program?

INFLUENTIAL AGENTS

People do not make their lifestyle choices in a vacuum. Because our lives are played out on a spiritual battlefield, in which a war rages around us and within us at all times, there are a wide variety of agents of influence that seek to persuade us to embrace one approach to life or the other; that is, to live for and in obedience to God, or to live for and in obedience to Satan. These are the only two sides at war and the only two choices we have, even though few people would ever characterize being oblivious to God or being disobedient to Him as meaning that they are serving Satan. It is politically incorrect to make such statements, but every human being has decided to be on one side or the other, whether the choice was intentional or not.

A constant battle exists in your mind, heart and soul. Consider the battle waged every time you enter a grocery store to buy a six-pack of soda. Prior to approaching the front lines (i.e., the grocery-store checkout line), you are exposed to a vicious war of propaganda, in which five or six brands tried to convince you that their product is best for you. You are exposed to multiple arguments—their brand is a better value, tastes better, is more socially acceptable, delivers a superior personal image—in the hope that one of those arguments would hit home and win your favor. Once you hit the battlefront, you have to declare your side and make one of the competitors the victor. You walk out of the store having spent your hard-earned money and feeling good about your choice of brand, which was, for all intents and purposes, no different from any other brand available to you.

Now expand that battle a millionfold in significance and intensity and recognize that's what happens in your life every moment of every day as God and Satan battle for your heart, mind and soul. Every seemingly minor choice you make—to give or withhold a compliment, to point out or remain silent regarding the error that's in your favor on the restaurant bill, whether or not to make a personal phone call on company time and at company expense, to ignore or pass along a rumor about a coworker's life, to donate or keep some spare change as you walk by a homeless person—represents another episode in the lifelong battle to affect your moral loyalty. As long as you are on this planet, the conflict will rage on as the apparent victor seeks to use you in the continual battle of good and evil, and as the apparent loser continues to maneuver in order to capture your allegiance.

What makes this argument seem preposterous to most Americans is that we cannot clearly see the battle, and most of us have never been properly informed about the nature of the battle—thinking that it does not affect us personally. When we watch a movie, we tend to think of it as either being satisfying or unsatisfying entertainment. However, a movie is much more than that. It is a weapon in the eternal conflict to either strengthen or weaken our worldview and our capacity to represent our side in the eternal war. We watched in wonder and horror as the Iraq War was waged in real time on our TV sets. And that's what we look for when someone speaks about the war between God and Satan (or good and evil)—a tangible, readily visible window on the war. In fact, one of the greatest victories won (so far) by God's enemy has been the ability to convince most people—even most Christians—that there is no war being waged, so we might as well relax, feel good and enjoy life.

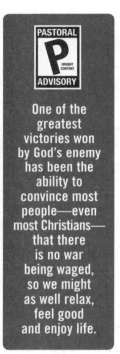

PASTORAL P URGENT CONTENT ADVISORY

One of the greatest victories won by God's enemy has been the ability to convince most people—even most Christians— that there is no war being waged, so we might as well relax, feel good and enjoy life.

Please know that the foundation of the war for people's souls, minds and hearts is waged against our children. If they can be persuaded when they are young, then it is incredibly difficult to change their allegiance as they age. And you, as a parent or spiritual leader, bear the primary responsibility for how that battle turns out.

Unfortunately, research we have conducted over the past several years regarding what influences people's choices suggests that God's agents of influence are not faring well. Attempting to ascertain what influences a person's thinking and behavior is extremely difficult. At best, we gain inferences into what seems to have the greatest impact on thought and behavior. Our efforts to determine levels of influence, however, have led us to some preliminary conclusions.

Conclusion 1: Three Tiers of Influence Exist

First, there seem to be three tiers of influence in American culture today. The relative influence of any particular element changes over the course of time, as society itself changes due to new technology, the impact of past influences and the ever-changing realities of spiritual warfare. In American society today, it appears that the most dominant agents of influence are contemporary music, movies (including videos and DVDs), television programming, the Internet, publications (dominated by books but including magazines and newspapers), laws and public policies, and parents. The second tier of influence agents includes peers, schools, radio, mentors, colleges and universities and siblings. The lower tier of influence encompasses churches and faith communities, adult education, counseling and therapy experiences, and extended family.[1] Naturally, the relative levels of influence vary from person to person, but these tiers appear to reflect what affects most kids in the 5- to 18-age category in America.

Conclusion 2: Levels of Influence Vary

Second, it is evident that the relative influence of these elements varies according to a person's age, life stage, family character and socioeconomic standing. In other words, parents have a much greater level of influence on a child who is two or three than do television and movies, but we find that the opposite is often true by the time the child is 16 years old. The rule of thumb we have arrived at is that parents are well advised to maximize their influence while the child is young. The older a child gets, the more distracted and vulnerable he or she becomes to nonfamily influences.

Conclusion 3: Foundations Develop Early

Third, various studies have confirmed the results of some of our data: By the age of nine, most of the moral and spiritual foundations of a child are in place. From the time a child is born until he or she is in the early primary grades, the child is voraciously consuming cues and lessons related to each of the developmental dimensions. It seems that by the time he or she is nine, the child shifts mental gears and begins to use the cues he or she receives from that point forward to either confirm or challenge an existing perspective.[2] It also appears that by the time the child has reached this age, it is much more difficult to change an existing view than to form a new view.

Conclusion 4: Validity of Views Is Continually Challenged

Fourth, even when young people have a defined perspective, every new experience causes them to challenge their prevailing views to some degree. We discovered that teenagers have a highly developed set of morals, values and beliefs. However, when they encounter something that conflicts with one of their perspectives, they will reconsider the validity of the view they hold. Whether they are ultimately willing to revise their viewpoint depends on various factors: the strength of their existing view, the degree of pressure from credible and reliable external sources, their own sense of discomfort with their view, the perceived benefits and how much of their resources would be consumed by reconsidering their position. Yet the possibility of change remains real, though less so as people age.

Conclusion 5: External Elements Influence

Fifth, most people deny that they are influenced by the elements of external influence enumerated earlier. Americans possess a charmingly simplistic notion that they are sensitive to efforts to influence their thinking and that they are vigilant in screening out undesirable influences. (That very idea, of course, begs the question of which influences initially penetrated their defenses to enable them to determine what is a good or bad influence.)

Conclusion 6: Intentional Effort Impacts

Finally, influencing a person's positions need not be intentional, but the more intentional and strategic the effort at influence is, the greater is the effect of that effort. In other words, you may influence someone without intending to or without realizing it, but such influence is real. However, when you focus on purposefully impacting someone's thoughts or behavior, the chances of having such an effect and of having the type of effect you hoped to have are increased substantially. Instead of having an accidental or unexpected degree of influence, you experience a more strategic impact on the person's life.

Afterthoughts from the Six Conclusions

I hope you picked up on a couple of key revelations from this research. For instance, did you notice that if you are a parent, you have a great degree of influence on a child, and such influence must be used strategically? Did you catch the notion that what you allow your child to ingest from mass media—movies, television, music, books and the Internet, in particular—probably has more cumulative impact than what you try to teach, thus making your role as the gatekeeper for media exposure enormously significant? And while I did not spell it out, perhaps you recognized the implication of the very limited influence that churches and church programs have on our young people. Such programs are not inherently bad or irrelevant, but the strategy of delivering our children to a church so that it can address children's moral and spiritual developmental needs is certainly flawed. Families—and parents, in particular—must invest in the moral and spiritual growth of their children with great concern, care and conscientiousness.

HELP

Often when parents and spiritual leaders try to influence kids, the goal is to impart proper information and provide feedback regarding behavior. We blend the proactive (imparting information that may eventually prove to be useful, either in a specific situation or in the development of more beliefs and values) with the reactive (applauding good behavior and reprimanding inappropriate behavior). Surveys among parents and spiritual leaders, however, indicate that few of these adults have a comprehensive view of what it might take to help young people grow into active, complete and passionate followers of Christ.

What do kids need? In essence, everything they need emanates from their worldview, so our challenge is to enable them to develop a biblical worldview, which is a means of interpreting and responding to reality that is consistent with God's ways as described for us in the Bible. In a previous book, I discussed the research we have conducted regarding worldview development—what a worldview is, the currently dominant worldviews in the United States and the seven questions that are most useful in helping to develop a biblical worldview.[3] For the purposes of this discussion, let me suggest that kids need our help with four Ps:

1. **P**urpose—identifying their purpose in life
2. **P**erspective—clarifying their core life perspectives

3. **P**rovision—providing basic conditions and benefits they need to grow in a healthy manner
4. **P**erformance—describing the performance of specific activities that enable them to lead productive and meaningful lives

Let's explore each of these areas.

PURPOSE

In our national research, we find that almost half of all adults say they are still seeking meaning and purpose in life. Among teenagers, 2 out of 3 are still seeking that sense of direction. Not surprisingly, the figures are highest among adolescents. We see this kind of confusion all around us, every day—people who meander through life, aimless and lethargic, capable but unproductive, comfortable but unfulfilled. That's a sure sign that even if they claim Jesus Christ as their Savior and acknowledge their existence as a gift from God, they do not understand why God created them.

Meaning and purpose in life are gained by developing spiritual understanding. Meaning and purpose are not all about occupational choices, educational degrees, marital status, financial security, personal achievement or leisure and recreational pursuits. It is about knowing God so intimately that you can discern His calling upon your life.

Establishing an unwavering commitment to God's calling should trump your devotion to realizing your personal desires every time (although when you consistently live for God, His desires eventually become indistinguishable from your desires). For instance, I've interviewed hundreds of people who have devoted themselves to trying to lead people, only to discover that they are unsuccessful and frustrated in their efforts. The reason for their ineffectiveness, though, is not that people are bad at taking direction but that perhaps the leader lacks the resources to fulfill the people's plans. In other words, the individual decided to be a leader even though God did not call him or her to be one. When you try to be something that God did not make you to be, you can count on a life of frustration, dissatisfaction and failure. When you listen to the voice of God to discern what He has called you to be, then you are in line for the blessings that enable you to succeed in the ventures for which He created you.

How, then, can we help children figure out God's calling for their lives; and what can we do to help young people begin to focus on God's purposes for their lives as early as possible?

Vision

The first step toward knowing that calling is to comprehend our life mission. The good news is that this is very easy to do, because we all have the same mission. The general description of life's purpose is perhaps best explicated in a conversation Jesus had with a professor of religion in Jerusalem:

> "You must love the Lord your God with all your heart, all your soul, all your strength, and all your mind." And, "Love your neighbor as yourself" (Luke 10:27, *NLT*).

As helpful as this is—reminding us that our lives are not our own—we live for the purpose of doing God's will—to bless Him and other people. Such a mission leaves us an awful lot of leeway as to *how* to love God and neighbor. When we are given broad instructions with little definition and guidance, we often find it hard to get focused and energized to identify and accomplish the real task God has set before us. That more specific aspect of our calling is the *vision* He has for us.

Whereas all believers share the same mission, God gives every true disciple of Jesus Christ a unique and detailed vision. If mission is generic, vision is very personal. It is God's idea of how you can be immersed in pursuing a different and better future that represents one of the building blocks of His kingdom. God calls each of us to commit to that vision—our calling—and prepares us for success in its pursuit by giving us the special combination of talents, skills, education, experiences, relationships and spiritual gifts required to bring that vision to reality.[4] Our calling defines the significant contribution that God has carved out for us to make to the Kingdom. And through our diligence in its pursuit, we will find meaning and joy in life. Our calling is one way in which God enables us to experience success according to His standards.

As you consider the children you are leading to become mature disciples of Christ, realize that you have the wonderful opportunity of helping them discern why God put them on Earth and how they can add value to His kingdom. That means assisting them in understanding and committing to God's mission and vision for their lives—His calling for them. As you reflect on how to empower children to grasp this pivotal revelation, keep in mind that their calling is composed of several facets that, when combined, produce an intense awareness of and commitment to that calling. Those components are purpose, passion, perseverance, power and pleasure.

Grasping the *Purpose*

As described above, God reveals His vision to us if we are willing to work with Him to grasp it. The sense of significance that vision provides us is irreplaceable. It is the missing link in the lives of most Christians—the absent bridge that prevents them from crossing from survival and salvation to sustainable significance. We come to discover that vision through a concerted time of intense prayer, vision-focused Bible study, situational analysis, self-awareness (with appropriate repentance, humility and self-confidence) and wise counsel. Together, these resources bring about a transformation in our understanding of life in general, and personal ministry in great detail.

Exploding with *Passion*

One way to know if we have truly ascertained God's vision for our lives is to evaluate our passion for that calling. Because the vision optimizes what God has invested in us, and because it is the opportunity to pursue something significant to God and His kingdom while simultaneously maximizing our personal resources, it should ignite tremendous excitement and energy. In interviews with thousands of people who have found their niche in the Kingdom by grasping God's vision for their lives, we have learned that they develop a sense of urgency about getting on target. In most cases, once people gain clarity about the vision, they not only burn with zeal, but they also cannot imagine being devoted to anything else in life. What else would provide them with such an opportunity to know God, serve God and bless God?

Strengthening *Perseverance*

A mark of God's purpose for our lives is that there is little chance of accomplishing that purpose based solely on our human capabilities. This incongruous situation—being called by God to a specific purpose that you are unable to fulfill—is by divine design. In such circumstances, we have no choice but to rely upon Him. If we had a life purpose that we could accomplish within divine intervention and empowerment, then who would need God? We must help our young ones to realize that God earnestly desires a meaningful and growing relationship with them. Consequently, He will provide them with a challenging calling that is beyond their grasp, which, therefore, will deepen their reliance upon Him.

Knowing that the calling is from Him and is thus tailor-made to our potential further strengthens us to resist and reject great opportunities that merely divert our attention and resources from our calling. Knowing with certainty what our life's purpose is enables us to muster the mental, moral and spiritual strength and self-confidence to keep moving ahead toward the fulfillment of what really matters.

Finding *Power*

When we are devoted to serving God according to our calling and rely upon Him for guidance and capacity, we will experience the power and the presence of God in our work. Remember, His vision exceeds our abilities; success only comes when we submit to His calling and allow Him to work through us, in us and around us in ways we cannot foresee or orchestrate. A common phrase uttered in response to a servant of God faithfully pursuing and seeing positive results is "Gee, I never thought she'd [he'd] be able to do that." The person could not have accomplished those feats without the presence and power of God at work in her or his life.

Experiencing *Pleasure*

People occasionally ask how we know if we have correctly understood God's calling. One of the most recognizable means is by experiencing pleasure and joy as we engage in that calling. Do not be misled, though. Serving God is not undertaken without suffering and struggle, but when we are doing His will in His way for His purposes, we will find a level of fulfillment unlike any we could otherwise experience in life.

As you work with kids, evaluate what brings them pleasure and fulfillment. It is likely that as they serve God, the activities that provide such meaning and enthrallment are somehow related to their calling.

Called Servants

Our research regarding ministry to children shows that churches recount the stories of great Bible heroes and amazing narratives, but they usually overlook the aspect of the calling that compelled each heroic Bible character to trust God and beat the odds. Let me identify a few of the spiritual heroes churches tend to teach about and God's special calling to each. Consider how well you have described the calling of these legendary individuals to the children to whom you relate as a parent or spiritual leader:

- Joseph, son of Jacob—called to rule Egypt and protect Israel (see Gen. 37:5-11; 50:20).

- Moses—called to rescue Israel, restore spiritual integrity and lead God's people to the Promised Land (see Exod. 3:7-10).

- Joshua—called to take control of the Promised Land and divide it fairly (see Josh. 1:1-9).

- Samuel—called to restore integrity to Israel and lead Israel's transition to a monarchy (see 1 Sam. 3; 7:5-6,15; 8:6-22).

- David—called to restore spiritual purity, peace and prosperity to Israel (see 1 Sam. 16:13; 1 Chron. 11:2).

- Solomon—called to build the Temple and rule Israel with wisdom (see 1 Kings 1:30-40).

- Josiah—called to restore Israel to spiritual purity and obedience (see 1 Kings 13:2).

- Ezekiel—called to challenge Israel to repent (see Ezek. 2:1—3:11).

- John the Baptist—called to prepare people for Jesus' coming (see Luke 1:13-17,76-79).

- Peter—called to establish and pastor churches among the Jews (see Matt. 16:18).

- Paul—called to evangelize and plant churches among the Gentiles (see Acts 9:1-30; 13:2-3; Rom. 15:20).

- Barnabas—called to be an itinerant teacher and encourager to those struggling with faith (see Acts 13:2).

Upon reading the life story of each of these servants, you will discover that He gave each of them special abilities to accomplish the specific calling He entrusted to him or her. These servants were convinced that their calling was significant and, therefore, of the utmost urgency. When the people who best knew the godly servants confirmed their calling as coming from God and being appropriate, the affirmation fueled a deeper sense of the importance of the call. Together, the servants' understanding of their gifts—a conviction that God instilled the gift for a special and urgent purpose—and the verification of others formed a powerful motivation in the servants to move forward in a unique and critical personal ministry.

What can you do to help the youngsters with whom you have contact discover God's purpose for their lives? As you explore their personality, spiritual gifts, passion, intellectual capacity, physical abilities, character traits and resonance with particular biblical characters and stories, funnel that knowledge toward guiding them to a clear idea of the role that has been reserved for them in God's army. Encourage them to feel neither arrogant nor disappointed by that role. No calling is better than any other, and if it is God's calling for them, then it is perfect for them.

Keep in mind that discerning the calling takes time, effort and sometimes a period of struggle or suffering. In other words, this is a process, not just a morning-long project. Be prepared to work alongside a child for a prolonged period of time as God unfolds the insights and experiences that will crystallize the calling in a way that generates ownership by the called individual.

PERSPECTIVE

Children need to know how to make sense of the world. From their earliest moments out of the womb, their brains are working furiously, trying to analyze the information that is pouring in and demanding interpretation and response. As children grow up, they develop mental categories that make such analysis and interpretation more efficient. Before they reach junior high, they have developed a worldview. That life lens enables them to quickly size up a situation and respond in ways that are consistent with what they believe is appropriate.

Unfortunately, most Americans develop their worldview by default. In other words, it is essentially learned through the sources of influence identified earlier. The alternative to worldview-by-default is for you, as a parent or spiritual leader, to intentionally and strategically lead a young person through a process designed to help the youth arrive at a worldview that is consistent with God's truths, principles and desires for His creation.

PASTORAL ADVISORY

Once the worldview of children has been shaped and embraced, they unconsciously strive to make choices that are consistent with their perspective.

Once the worldview of children has been shaped and embraced, they unconsciously strive to make choices that are consistent with their perspective. To do otherwise raises internal dissonance, which brings discomfort and a sense of being lost. Many of the battles that we fight in our culture today—battles related to personal values, public policies and laws, individual behavior and religious beliefs and practices—are predictable and inevitable given the worldviews that people possess. If we want to transform our society so that it honors God, we must address the worldview that most young people embrace. They are prone to behavior that is consistent with their beliefs, and their beliefs are the result of their worldview.

The notion of helping others develop a biblical worldview seems daunting to many parents and spiritual leaders. It need not be, though. We start with an understanding of what resources are required to facilitate such an outcome. Four cornerstones exist, which need to be identified and used in order to help children build a solid foundation.

Cornerstone 1: The Bible

We rely upon the Bible as a credible source of wisdom in our reflections as to how to think and respond. God may use other means of enlightening us as to what is appropriate (i.e., insights drawn from tradition, experience or direct revelation); but any insight, regardless of its point of origin, must be consistent with Scripture. As a coach in this worldview process, your challenge is to raise the young person's acceptance of and reliance upon Scripture as a trustworthy source of direction and wisdom. You must confirm this through your personal dependence upon God's Word for daily guidance.

Cornerstone 2: A Commanding Knowledge of Biblical Content

Millions of Americans contend that the Bible is inspired by God, accurate in substance and helpful in practice, but they never open the pages to glean its value for their own lives! Your challenge is to lead children not only to endorse the Bible as a good book but also to know its teachings so well that they can readily call upon its principles in any given situation. Teach them in a way that connects the biblical principles with their personal life circumstances and cultural leanings. Identifying critical passages of Scripture for them to know and even memorize—not just John 3:16 and a parcel of other core evangelistic verses, or a series of esoteric passages that reflect profound wisdom, but also a few dozen integrated verses that provide comprehensive insight into life—is a significant step.

Cornerstone 3: The Identification of Organizing Principles

Our research finds that most churches teach good biblical content but fail to tie it together into a logical and comprehensive framework that makes sense and provides practical counsel. People get overwhelmed with the amount of Bible-based information delivered and, lacking an understanding of how it all fits together, pick and choose what they like or what seems most relevant to their current circumstances, discarding the rest. Instead, you can assist young people in connecting the dots of God's principles so that they draw a striking picture of truth and purpose without getting lost down the rabbit trails of spiritual intrigue. Naturally, once you have helped them to determine the organizing principles and associated insights, you must reinforce that perspective through your personal reliance upon those principles in the development and application of the biblical worldview in your own life.

Cornerstone 4: A Burning Desire to Obey God

Motivating children to have a burning desire to obey God, as facilitated through the application of their worldview, is not merely an intellectual exercise designed to reflect a high view of Scripture or to reflect substantial exposure to biblical teaching. Our worldview is the springboard to our children's behavior. If we profess to be followers of Jesus Christ, then our worldview should demonstrate a commitment to His principles and standards as manifested in our daily choices and actions.

Your challenge is to motivate young people to have a thirst for the righteousness of God; that is, to always do what is right in God's eyes because they want nothing more than to honor and please Him. Serving as a mentor and accountability partner for the youths entrusted to you is a vital link in the process of shaping their worldview. Encouraging them when they do well is a critical element in reinforcing their efforts to love God with all their heart, mind, strength and soul.

The Integration of the Four Cornerstones

But what is the content of a biblical worldview? Is it unrealistic to believe that a parent or lay leader or, perhaps, even a pastor or church staffer who sees a child just an hour or two each week could possibly infuse something as profound and massive as a worldview into a young person's mind, heart and spirit?

No, this process can be readily accomplished if we put the cornerstones in place, commit to the process and approach worldview development through the application of a simple set of organizing principles. I suggest that your organizing principles be a series of seven questions that you work with children to answer and apply through your interaction with them. Raising these questions, rather than simply telling stories and requiring memorization, forces them to think (i.e., we don't tell them the answers), provides them with a sense of ownership of their worldview (because they arrived at the answers) and facilitates personal application of those perspectives far better than concepts proposed by a teacher.

The choice of questions for students to ponder is critical since the substance of those questions either helps in the development of a useful and biblically consistent worldview or causes confusion. Having studied this process, I suggest that you process the following seven questions with the children to whom you minister:

1. Does God exist?
2. What is the character and nature of God?
3. How and why was the world created?
4. What is the nature and purpose of humanity?
5. What happens after we die on Earth?
6. What spiritual authorities exist?
7. What is truth?

These questions take us from the beginning of eternity to its end and touch on everything of significance in between those time-space bookends. I have written more extensively elsewhere about the nature and substance of the answers to these questions.[5] If you don't like these questions, develop your own set of queries that you are confident will enable a person to think biblically, comprehensively, insightfully and practically in regard to any moral, ethical, relational, financial, political or spiritual situation in which they find themselves.

Experience has shown that this process is best conducted as an open-ended dialogue rather than a series of lectures. Children need to be taught the fundamental biblical principles and truths that underlie the answers to these questions, but they also need to stretch their imaginations and envision personal applications in ways that transcend the recitation of stock replies. The goal is to help them grasp a way of thinking rather than a parcel of quotations that seem disconnected from personal reality.

PROVISION

Fostering spiritual transformation demands that we do our best to eliminate some of the emotional and behavioral obstacles to growth. If children are consumed by fears and worries regarding safety and capacity, little growth can occur.

A key element to consider is emotional security. Various studies have shown that until children feel loved, accepted, affirmed and engaged, there is limited hope of seeing significant progress in their development.

Various studies have shown that until children feel loved, accepted, affirmed and engaged, there is limited hope of seeing significant progress in their development.

The family is the most important player in this drama. Conversation, activity and values that promote emotional security set the stage for spiritual development.

Another factor to address is that of empowering children to grow. While the term "empowerment" has been much abused in recent years, we can enhance the likelihood of children growing spiritually when they are confident of physical safety and interpersonal acceptance, and senses that the roles they play are useful and appropriate. We find that young people feel empowered when they are able to see themselves as significant human beings (based on a combination of positive self-image and their perception that others deem them to be important and valuable), are able to act in a self-governed manner and feel that they are a contributing value to their community. Adding value to their world is achieved by giving them opportunities to use their skills and gifts, enabling them to work as members of a team and facilitating meaningful interaction between mentors and children. Thus, the facilitator's role enables such perspectives and behaviors to emerge.

A further condition that adults must facilitate for young people is a viable process of accountability. Personal experience confirms what the Bible teaches: Without commitment to structures and relationships that establish boundaries and hold us to certain limitations, our sin nature drives us to ignore such restrictions, no matter how healthy or sensible those contours may be. Personal experience also helps us to understand that such parameters are neither easy to establish and enforce nor bound to make us popular. Yet they are one of the most significant benefits we can add to the lives of children. The absence of such discipline leaves children open to all kinds of destructive possibilities, including self-destruction.

PERFORMANCE

As we build these assets and resources into the lives of children, we must remember that this is not simply for the purpose of doing good works or providing a positive developmental environment. Our ultimate goal is to build a spiritual foundation that serves as the basis of children's human development. In the process, we can enable young people to optimize their spiritual foundation by helping them to experience and grow their faith in tangible, practical ways. To do so, we must address the children's involvement in the six pillars of Christian formation: worship, evangelism, discipleship, stewardship, service and community.

Worship

Amazingly, our research finds that most born-again adults have little understanding of genuine worship. Most believers think of worship as an event they attend, a type of music that relates to faith matters or a practice that primarily provides personal benefit. To be spiritually whole, children need a mature believer who will help them discover the awesome reality of authentically and intimately connecting with God by providing what He deserves, demands and delights in—heartfelt worship. This practice goes far beyond attending weekly events. Young people must come to understand their lives as a constant exercise of worship. Practicing and enjoying God's presence, while maintaining a respect and awe for who He is, is one of the enormous challenges we face in raising our children.

Evangelism

The Great Commission is no less daunting or necessary today than it was when Jesus first spoke these words to His followers: "Therefore go and make disciples of all nations, baptizing them in the name of the Father and of the Son and of the Holy Spirit, and teaching them to obey everything I have commanded you. And surely I am with you always, to the very end of the age" (Matt. 28:19-20). Every believer is charged with the responsibility of sharing the good news of what Jesus Christ has done for every human through His suffering on the cross and His resurrection.

Equipping young people to not only embrace Jesus as their Lord and Savior but also to accept His call to spread the news to those who are not yet eternally connected to Him through His grace is a privilege. Encouraging them to confidently share their faith in Jesus with friends—and to do so with humility, discernment, wisdom, love and boldness—is often easier said than done. However, for years our research has shown that kids are more comfortable sharing their faith than are adults. Our responsibility is to prepare and encourage them and then see how the Holy Spirit uses them in the process.

Discipleship

Discipling children can be one of the more common and fun aspects of facilitating their development. In some ways, though, we are not sufficiently conscientious about the process. Often, kids receive spiritual teaching when it is convenient for parents or when on a regimented schedule (e.g., every Sunday), without a lifelong, moment-to-moment process. Our job is to lead children to develop a habit of continual spiritual growth through prayer, Bible study, service and the various spiritual disciplines. Some parents have learned that seeing themselves as their children's personal spiritual coach helps them to view common experiences and everyday circumstances as the training grounds on which to foster spiritual development.

Stewardship

Training children to be good managers of the resources God entrusts to them—the process typically referred to as stewardship—may be a broader task than expected. The resources over which we have immediate dominion—money, relationships, ideas, skills, spiritual gifts, time and possessions—are so pervasive that our training in the dimension of stewardship may need to be more diligent. Most children indicate that they receive teaching and encouragement concerning how to use their money but that they are rarely challenged in terms of how they manage God's other resources. We would serve children well by providing them with a more intentional focus upon how to effectively administer *all* resources for God's purposes and in accordance with His principles.

Service

One of the best ways for people to develop their faith is by serving people. It becomes unhealthy for Christians to get in the routine of attending church events and taking spiritual resources from those activities while failing to give away whatever they have received, whether those resources are tangible or intangible. The Christian faith is not meant to be hoarded but shared. Our faith is founded on the notion of expressing love in real ways, not simply discussing it as an intellectual concept. Building the habit of service at a young age tends to alter the attitudes and expectations of young people, resulting in a lifelong practice of helping others. The younger we instill such a mind-set and lifestyle, the more ingrained they become.

Community

The final practice that we must facilitate for our children is that of engagement in a community of believers, where they are accepted, instructed, encouraged, supported and held accountable. Assisting children in connecting emotionally and spiritually with other children and in accepting the rules of the community in relation to faith principles is an invaluable discipline. In a culture in which moral anarchy is increasingly the standard, immersing our young people in an alternative system of relationships and responsibilities is one of the most important challenges we face for their personal health, the good of the Church and the hope of the nation at large.

THE CHALLENGE

If you were to honestly express your feelings at this moment, after reading the various tasks and responsibilities outlined in this chapter, you might feel overwhelmed and underskilled to do the job described. Have no fear—you are not alone and you are not incapable of mastering this challenge!

Most Christian parents and even those who take on assignments regarding children's spiritual development feel as if they are incapable of making much headway. Our studies reveal that most parents don't feel that they have sufficient spiritual maturity to provide the kind of comprehensive education and training described in this chapter. Sometimes that sense of personal inadequacy results in "lowering the bar"—that is, setting the standard just a wee bit above what we have achieved in our own lives rather than seeking to maximize our children's true potential in Christ.

If you feel the least bit inadequate or overwhelmed, let me encourage you to put your feelings in perspective.

If we were to assess how well Jesus or Paul discipled people, we'd have to admit that the outcomes were surprisingly imperfect. The followers of Christ in the Early Church fought, drank, misused their money, gossiped, committed adultery and used profane language. In short, they were people just like us. Certainly we don't want to use these outcomes as an excuse for us to take an "anything goes" attitude, but we must remember that we are sinful people trying to help other sinners in a culture that facilitates sin. No matter how much we love God and our own children, we will do an imperfect job of raising spiritual champions.

That's why we have to remember that it is not we who cause transformation but the Holy Spirit working through us that brings about such inner change. Our responsibility is not to do it all and to perform with perfection but to be available and diligent in our personal spiritual growth and to be willing to invest in the spiritual growth of our children. God will do the rest, sometimes through us and sometimes in spite of us.

Also remember that the Church exists to support us in our efforts to raise our children in ways that honor God and advance His kingdom. We cannot legitimately pawn off our kids on a church and expect it to do the job we as parents have been given by God. However, we can partner with the church to compensate for our own areas of developmental weakness or inability so that our children mature into dynamic followers of Christ. Working in tandem with other believers is one of the marks of a healthy Christian and a healthy community of faith.

Every one of us wants our children to grow up to be great spiritual men or women. But getting there is a struggle. Remember, we're immersed in a war, and making progress in war is always a hardship. Helping our children to develop spiritually is a journey of faith, not a destination we can expect to reach by some predictable or designated point in time. When

Paul wrote that we must fight the good fight of faith, he may well have had the raising of spiritual children in mind, knowing that it's harder to stand fast for what is right and true than to settle for what is easy and popular. Be encouraged that those of us who resist the temptation to give up or slough off and who persevere with every last ounce of strength because we know that the spiritual development of our young ones matters to God, will be blessed for our effort by the One who calls each of us to reflect His image in all that we say, think and do.

CHAPTER 5

TAKING ON APPROPRIATE RESPONSIBILITY

Parents across the nation admit that one of the greatest benefits they receive from attending a church is having that community of faith assume responsibility for the spiritual development of their children. Knowing that there are trained professionals and other willing individuals who will provide spiritual guidance to their children is a source of security and comfort for most churchgoing adults.

Our national surveys have shown that while more than 4 out of 5 parents (85 percent) believe they have the primary responsibility for the moral and spiritual development of their children, more than two out of three of them abdicate that responsibility to their church. Their virtual abandonment of leading their children spiritually is evident in how infrequently they engage in faith-oriented activities with their young ones. For instance, we discovered that in a typical week, fewer than 10 percent of parents who regularly attend church with their kids read the Bible together, pray together (other than at meal times) or participate in an act of service as a family unit. Even fewer families—

Fewer than 10 percent of parents who regularly attend church with their kids read the Bible together, pray together or participate in an act of service as a family unit.

1 out of every 20—have any type of worship experience together with their kids, other than while they are at church during a typical month.

In short, most families do not have a genuine spiritual life together. However, we also found that this is not disturbing to most of them for two reasons. First, they are merely following the precedent that was set for them. In other words, American parents—even those who are born-again churchgoers described by their church as "pillars"—are generally doing what their parents did with them: dropping off the kiddies at church and allowing the religious professionals to mastermind the spiritual development of the young people. No matter how much church leaders preach about the need for parents to personally invest in the spiritual growth of children, adults tend to revert to what was modeled for them, noting that carting the kids to church and occasional religious events is sufficient. "After all," explained one mother, echoing a sentiment that has become a very common reply emerging from our research, "that's what my parents did with me and I turned out pretty good." This notion of turning out "pretty good" is especially widespread among Baby Boomers.

Second, most churchgoing parents are neither spiritually mature nor spiritually inclined and, therefore, they do not have a sense of urgency or necessity about raising their kids to be spiritual champions. Most parents believe that enabling their children to attend church on a regular basis and to feel generally positive about their religious experience is as high as they can set the bar. Anything achieved beyond that level is seen as a bonus.

But how do parents reconcile the apparent contradiction between saying that they have the primary responsibility for the spiritual development of their children and their practice of dropping off the kids for others to provide virtually all of the spiritual instruction that their children receive? By believing that *because* they are responsible and yet personally incapable of meeting their children's spiritual needs, the best thing they can do is to seek the help of others who are more skilled in spiritual matters. Based on their upbringing and the prevailing cultural assumptions, they believe that their church is the best provider of spiritual nurturing for their kids—a solution to meeting the spiritual needs of their children that is viewed by these parents as a reasonable, best-hope resort.

Once again, there is some merit to their assumptions. Our research shows that a minority of parents of young children believe that they are doing a good job of shaping the moral and spiritual beliefs of their youngsters—a perspective confirmed by more than 4 out of 5 adults who observe the performance of those parents. All types of reasons are given by these parents for their lack of ability: the complexity of modern life, the inescapable negative influence of the media, the distorting views and behaviors of their children's peers, the warped perspectives taught in the schools, the lack of trust children have in their parents' moral and spiritual perspectives, the cultural reinforcement of unbiblical thought and behavioral patterns, the ingrained nature of the politically correct movement, and so forth. Essentially, parents have used these reasons to convince themselves that they cannot do any better than they are doing because they are overmatched.

The common response to the spiritual development of children, then, is for parents to seek the best help they can find and then get out of the way. That's exactly what most parents do—and they are generally quite pleased with the results. Almost 9 out of 10 parents of pre-teens (87 percent) say they are satisfied with the quality of ministry and counsel their young ones receive from their church.

TABLE 5.1

AN EVALUATION OF HOW PARENTS ARE DOING IN RAISING THEIR CHILDREN

Description of upbringing technique	Doing an excellent/good job according to other churched adults	How parents of churched kids under 13 rate themselves
Helping the child to develop a world-view based on the Bible	22%	64%
Providing regular spiritual instruction and experiences	24	72
Identifying and consistently enforcing standards of behavior	26	80
Nurturing the child's relationship with God	27	72
Providing opportunities to serve the community or nation	27	60
Giving the child sufficient personal attention each day	31	81
Training the child to have marketable skills	33	63
Providing a stable emotional environment	35	87
Providing exposure to current trends in thought and lifestyle	37	60
Trusting the child	39	81
Helping the child to have high self-esteem	42	88
Facilitating good friendships	43	87
Providing a safe and stable physical environment	53	93
Enabling the child to get a good formal education	56	87
Loving the child	66	97

Source: Barna Research Group national surveys among 1,003 adults, conducted 2002.

THE PROBLEM OF THE COMPLIANT CHURCH

Churches, of course, are pleased to have people relying upon them for help. After all, they exist for that very reason. The inflow of families enables the Church to provide an even broader array of programs and services thanks to the economies of scale and the momentum produced by having larger numbers of people involved.

Thus, parents are happy, children receive some religious instruction and experiences, and churches are serving people. This sounds like a wonderful win-win situation except for one issue: *The approach is completely unbiblical!*

When a church—intentionally or not—assumes a family's responsibilities in the arena of spiritually nurturing children, it fosters an *unhealthy dependence* upon the church to relieve the family of its biblical responsibility. We should be careful to not be too harsh on churches, for there are many situations in which a child's family will have nothing to do with spiritual development. In those cases, a child must depend on the church to provide lessons in faith or he or she will essentially go without spiritual training. And there are millions of families who have a proper relationship with their church, providing spiritual direction and training to their child that is supplemented by their church. That is a very desirable situation—the family takes the lead in the process, and the church supports its efforts.

God's plan is for families to lead in the provision of spiritual development for their children.

However, our research shows that it is the rare church that possesses such insight into a young person's family situation. Most churches simply enroll kids within a program when they show up; and the churches may not have—or even seek to have—any contact with the family whatsoever, apart from encouraging the parents to attend the church and to keep bringing their children. Thus, a majority of churches are actually guilty of perpetuating an unhealthy and unbiblical process wherein the church usurps the role of the family and creates an unfortunate and sometimes exclusive dependency upon the church for a child's spiritual nourishment.

THE CLARITY OF THE BIBLE

God's plan is for families to lead in the provision of spiritual development for their children. Churches certainly have a viable role in that process—as will be discussed in the next chapter—but it is parents who will be held accountable by God for the spiritual growth of their offspring.

In fact, the Bible provides a simple and clear notion of what the family ought to do to raise godly children:

- *Parents should provide the primary spiritual training of children.* The parents may receive encouragement, training and resources through the Church, but the parents are intended by God to be the primary provider of spiritual direction and care (see Deut. 1:31; 6:4-9; 11:18-21; 21:18-19; Ps. 78:5-8; Luke 8:39; Eph. 6:4).

- *The purpose of spiritual training is to instill a passion to love, obey and serve God.* The outcome is not mere knowledge but also true wisdom and discernment as evidenced in behavior (see Matt. 10:37; 12:48-50; 1 Tim. 4:7; 2 Tim. 3:15-17).

- *Parents must start the spiritual training of children when they are young.* Waiting too long produces unfortunate outcomes for parents and children (see Isa. 7:15; Acts 26:4).

- *Worshiping God is one of a believer's most significant responsibilities.* Parents must lead their family together in regular worship of God (see Deut. 16:11; 29:18; 1 Sam. 1:19).

- *Spiritual development is a lifelong, continual process.* It is not to be practiced as a once-a-week routine, but a 24/7 habit. Even after children leave home, the parents retain the obligation to look after the spiritual life of their offspring in the hope of someday presenting them to God as mature and obedient servants (see Deut. 6:7; 11:19; Prov. 22:6).

- *Part of the parental responsibility is to introduce appropriate discipline into children's lives and to avoid pampering them.* This encompasses spiritual discipline as well as parameters in other parts of life (see Prov. 3:11-12; 13:1,24; 19:18; 23:12-14; 29:15-17,21; Col. 3:20).

- *Parents are called to introduce their children to appropriate behavior, as modeled by the Church's patriarchs and saints* (see Num. 18:11; Deut. 15:20; 16:11).

- *Spiritual transformation requires us to rely upon God's grace and power; we must therefore pray for the children we seek to impact for God* (see 1 Sam. 1:10-16; 2 Sam. 12:16; Lam. 2:19).

- *The basis of spiritual training is the Bible.* Parents are instructed to rely upon it for truth, values, principles and direction as they nurture their children (see Prov. 30:5; Matt. 4:4; 21:16; Mark 12:24; Rom. 15:3-4; 2 Tim. 3:15).

- *The family will grow in spiritual maturity as it serves God and people as a family unit* (see Gen. 7—9; Exod. 27:21—30:30; Josh. 24:15).

- *Young people will retain childish perspectives and reasoning unless their parents help them grow beyond such limited thinking* (see Prov. 17:21; 1 Cor. 13:11).

- *Parents are encouraged to work in tandem with reliable spiritual partners—such as the Church—but should be sure that those partners are committed to the things of God* (see 1 Sam. 1:27-28; 3:1-10; Rom. 14:19; Eph. 4:11-13).

- *The worldview of children should be shaped after the worldview of the parents* (see Luke 6:40).

- *The father is charged with passing on the spiritual blessing to the children.* That duty is a serious transfer of God's blessing upon the family and cannot be received through any other means or persons (see Gen. 27; 2 Sam. 6:20; 1 Chron. 16:43).

- *Before God will hand over great spiritual responsibility to an adult who has children, the parent must give proof of being a dedicated and effective parent* (see 1 Tim. 3:4-5,12).

GEORGE BARNA

In a nutshell, then, parents have a simple but profound responsibility to evangelize and disciple their children. The local church should be an intimate and valuable partner in the effort to raise the coming generation of Christ's followers and church leaders, but it is the parents whom God will hold primarily accountable for the spiritual maturation of their children.

And keep this lesson in mind, too: Every encounter with another person, including children, results in the transmission of influence. You may do things that influence your children, or your children may do things that influence you. To leave a positive imprint on the children you interact with, be sensitive to who is influencing whom—and toward what end.

The Raising of a Spiritual Champion

In the effort to evangelize and disciple their children, parents are given carte blanche by Scripture in regard to the methods that can be used to raise godly children. There is no infallible approach to effectively motivate and teach children to be godly. Just as every church has a different vision and context for its ministry and will approach how it ministers differently as a result of its uniqueness, so will every family approach parenting in ways that fit their style, relationships and calling from God.

Having noted the freedom that God provides us in parenting, though, let me also remind you that there are very specific values, beliefs and outcomes that honor—and do not honor—God. Our research has explored the approach to fostering godliness and spiritual maturity in children. Let me briefly outline the various methods of instruction being widely used—not because you will necessarily learn something new (you are probably aware of all of these methods), but to remind you of the full arsenal of tools God has provided for the task He has assigned to you.

Behavioral Modeling

I start with behavioral modeling because our research suggests it is the most powerful component in a parent's efforts to influence a child. It appears that as our society becomes increasingly secular, our children are developing a hypocrisy detector—an internal sensitivity to actions, attitudes, values and beliefs that are inherently contradictory to words that have been uttered as instructions. When an inconsistency is identified, a child is prone to do two things: (1) ignore the instruction itself; and (2) conclude that there is no specific command that they must obey.

Perhaps you have discovered the same truth that has awakened many parents: Raising children pushes parents to mature in their faith as much as it moves children toward spiritual wholeness. If you are struggling with particular aspects of raising your child, especially in relation to the faith dimension, step back and evaluate your behavior. You may discover that while you are able to voice the appropriate concepts to your young ones, your behavior negates those words. The "do as I say, not as I do" approach is increasingly incompatible with effective influence upon children.

Raising children pushes parents to mature in their faith as much as it moves children toward spiritual wholeness.

Conversely, we have discovered that many parents are not effective at verbally articulating the values, attitudes, beliefs and lifestyle they want their children to embrace, but their own behavior so consistently displays those elements that their kids naturally follow suit. In these situations, our actions do speak louder than any words we offer. (Of course, we also find that verbal instruction backed by consistent action is a powerful one-two punch that often leads to imitation by children.)

Formal Instruction

Many adults assume that for children to grow, the parents (or other authority figures) must verbalize a lesson or command. It is common for parents to orchestrate dedicated times for teaching predetermined lessons, whether those moments focus on sexual values, money matters, relational principles or other matters designed to further the moral and spiritual character of their children. In addition, parents try to stay alert to teachable moments that arise unexpectedly but provide moments of opportunity to make a point or reinforce a point previously made.

Simply talking at children (i.e., lecturing them) often proves to have less impact, however, than does combining the power of presentation with other educational strategies. For instance, making a presentation interactive—by asking children questions about the concept or situation, or asking for their reaction or personal experience related to the concept—involves the children in the learning process. Such two-way communication leads the children to own the outcomes of the dialogue as personal insights rather than someone else's wisdom that they are welcome (or expected) to embrace. The more capable you are of inciting your children to consider, analyze and draw conclusions regarding the concepts, the more likely they will internalize those outcomes and permanently hold on to the lesson.

Another teaching tool that helps many parents is their willingness to tell personal stories and integrate some degree of personal vulnerability into their narrative in order to capture attention and drive home a point. This process has to be handled adroitly, because if the children sense that the adult has no real mastery of the subject or has not grown as a result of the situation described, then the parents lose the perceived authority required to impart the truths and principles in question. When parents effectively describe a compelling life event that resulted in personal transformation, children are more likely to glean valuable wisdom from the story.

Reading

Raising children in the era of video expression—movies, videos, DVDs, video games, cable television, PowerPoint presentations, Internet surfing and instant messaging—has reduced the appeal of reading. However, our research demonstrates that while the reading skills of the typical child have deteriorated over recent decades, most kids do spend time reading on a regular basis. The challenge for parents is to sell their kids on reading material that will be both interesting and instructive.

Parents who say that there is no reading matter that captures their children's imagination or that adequately conveys desired lessons to their kids probably have not done their homework. Every year there are more than 140,000 new titles published in the United States. The Christian publishing industry adds thousands of new titles each year, and juvenile books represent one of the faster growing sectors of the industry. Add to these books the numerous magazines, newsletters, CD-ROMs, video games and Internet sites available, and it is hard to imagine the absence of a resource to meet any particular need, interest, perspective or grade level.

Creative Applications

In my travels around the world, I have noticed that Americans are often so busy that they take little, if any, time to reflect on their experiences. Some parents have tried to counteract such superficiality by having their children write about the lessons they learn. The act of writing often forces people to organize and clarify their thoughts, helping them to make greater sense of the information in question.

Parents who have gotten their children to keep spiritual diaries often report that after the initial wave of resistance, kids get into the process of recording what God is doing in their lives, or the kinds of questions and ruminations they harbor regarding spiritual matters. Parents have used the diary process in various ways: as a discussion starter for family devotions or conversations regarding faith, as a means of initiating dialogue about spiritual issues that are unclear to the child, and as a way of helping the child to see how God is at work in the child's life.

Another approach taken by some families—especially those involved in homeschooling—is to assign a paper, akin to a school report, in which children write their feelings, impressions, insights or reactions to a passage of Scripture or a personal experience. These essays are most useful when children share the content with their families as an article of discussion—not so much as a product to be critiqued, but as a step of faith to be further explored and considered. Essays that produce personal action are especially useful for the writer.

Personal Experiences

Because of the fact that there are different types of learners (e.g., visual, kinesthetic and auditory), some children will grow most profoundly by having a firsthand experience that illustrates a principle or truth. (Frankly, we have found that most children learn through experiences—either having an eye-opening lesson or having a previously grasped lesson clarified and reinforced.)

Our research among the current crop of young people (i.e., the postmodern generations) suggests that shared experiences are among the most successful teaching episodes. Teenagers and adolescents, who tend to move about with their relational tribe of 4 to 12 individuals, often rely on experiences to provide their defining moments. Whether the experiences are intentionally orchestrated to deliver a lesson or emerge spontaneously, the effect can be profound.

From a spiritual vantage point, parents are well advised to consider how to make Bible study, worship, community service projects and prayer times more than a predictable, scheduled intrusion on their children's schedules. Debriefing young people after such experiences may enhance the experience (or future experiences) by introducing greater introspection and analysis. (For the adult, such feedback provides useful nuggets of insight into how future experiences might be more instructive.)

Discipline

One of the most underutilized resources available to parents—and which should be among the most often-used resources—is that of discipline. This form of instruction includes the identification of parameters and expectations, assistance in developing proper habits, situational reprimands and friendly reminders. The Bible makes it quite clear that discipline is an expression of love—and that the failure or refusal to utilize discipline is tantamount to withholding love (see Prov. 1:7; 6:23; 13:24; 19:18; 22:15; 29:15; 29:17; Eph. 6:4; Heb. 12:8-11).

Method Combination

Research we have conducted related to effective instruction shows that the impact on a child is multiplied by incorporating a variety of methods to get the job done. Reliance upon a single method becomes predictable and boring. Even developing a regimented rotation of methods becomes ineffective once the student tires of the pattern and forced technique. Parents and teachers maximize their impact when they have enough self-confidence to use whatever approach seems right for the child and the lesson to be imparted.

THE WISDOM OF EXPERIENCE

Children are not the only ones who learn as parents try to teach their kids spiritual realities. Sometimes parents learn spiritual truths, which advance their own Christlikeness. Other times they discover insights related to effective instruction. The oft-repeated bits of wisdom given below were learned by parents the hard way—through experience.

Get Your Priorities Straight

One of the lessons that wiser parents than I have learned is to remember that God cares a lot less about what we achieve that draws applause from the world—how many consecutive profitable quarters we led the corporation to amass, how clean and organized we kept our home or how many educational degrees we piled up—than how we raise our children. As a prolific list maker—yes, I am among the world's greatest practitioners of the to-do list—I froze in my tracks one day while reading the transcripts of some of our interviews with parents, several of whom noted that their to-do list was chock full of tasks to complete before hitting the sack but that the list completely overlooked anything they hoped to accomplish with their kids that day. Already aware of the result, I slowly glanced at my list for that day and found that I was the epitome of the productive executive who claimed his kids were a top priority but whose carefully defined daily agenda made no mention of desired outcomes related to his children.

You're probably not as uptight as I am about daily productivity, but that's not the point. As you concoct your daily schedule, where do your kids fit in that framework? Unless they are acknowledged as a top priority and there are specific outcomes we hope to achieve with them and will work to facilitate, the chance of accomplishing significant influence with them is significantly reduced. Think about the household chores, sales calls, bill paying, meal preparation or whatever it is that is important to you. Do you leave those items to chance or do you make a point of prioritizing the behaviors that lead to those nonnegotiable outcomes?

Apply that same logic to your parenting efforts. If you believe that your children's spiritual nurturing is a critical responsibility and that you must be intentional about such growth, shouldn't one or a few specific actions that advance the spiritual development of your children be at the top of your to-do list?

Give It Up—Whatever It Is

The age-old expression Nothing good comes easy, contains much wisdom. In relation to the raising of spiritual champions, we need to recognize that the resistance and hardship that we experience in attempting to help our young ones grow are inevitable. As part of the spiritual war for their minds, hearts and souls, we know that there are spiritual adversaries arrayed against us. As people seeking to introduce righteousness and holiness into a fallen world and within a culture that revels in darkness, being different will bring its share of challenges. In a world that treasures position, possessions and pleasure, the notion of sacrificing personal rewards and opportunities for the benefit of the spiritual growth of children is frowned upon. This is yet another challenge we must confront: Is the spiritual development of our children significant enough to us that we are willing to give up some of our own possibilities for the sake of the young ones?

Be a Parenting Team

Another challenge to families is that of each parent's making the time and working in harmony with his or her spouse to facilitate spiritual growth among the children. Most families that have young children also have both the mother and father working outside of the home. Even in those families in which one of the parents does not work outside the home, the challenge is for the parents to work in a complementary fashion, adding value to the child-rearing process beyond a single contribution (e.g., one spouse makes the money, the other manages the household).

As the cultural context for child development becomes more complicated, it is imperative that the husband and wife work as a dynamic duo—"dynamic" in the sense of working together to exhibit flexibility and a willingness to add value to what their partner brings to the table.

The more the parents plan their respective inputs to the developmental process, the better off the children will be—not because the developmental process is more efficient, but because there has been strategic forethought invested in that process.

Let me add a word about single parents. Obviously, they have an incredibly difficult job. Seeking to establish all the requisite building blocks, including spiritual strength, in their children's lives is a massive and exhausting undertaking that is not meant for a single human being to take on. We found examples of single parents partnering with other single parents (and, in some cases, two-parent families) to try to team teach their kids whatever they need.

Earn the Right

One of the common barriers to spiritual development arises when parents or teachers assume that by virtue of their age and life status they should be granted the authority to teach moral and spiritual truths to children. However, we find that children do not afford adults unlimited or unquestioned authority to instruct them. Initially, adults have the opportunity to provide moral and spiritual lessons simply because they are adults. After a short while, though, children are able to assess the spiritual integrity of the adults in their lives. From that point forward, the adult must *earn the right* to flex that authority.

Most of the parents we interviewed contended that because they have the position, they always have the authority to provide moral and spiritual instruction. Whether that is legitimate or not, the fact is that children live in a society that requires teachers to demonstrate that they are worthy of a child's consideration. When your children look past your assigned role to ponder your spiritual integrity, what do they see?

Provide Continuity

One of the frequent obstacles to spiritual development is the lack of continuity that children experience. Perhaps we start to move down a track of training but fail to finish the course. Maybe we examine the facts of a Bible story with our kids but fail to discuss the personal implications of the story's principles. Sometimes we encourage and applaud certain behavior from our kids for a period of time, but after a while we become oblivious or distracted and stop reinforcing that activity, thus sending a mixed message. In our lust for the latest and greatest, we are apt to ignore the lessons of the past and fail to explore our connections to the historic Church.

Have you noticed that these days there is little sense of spiritual heritage that gets passed from one generation of believers to the next? Select almost any section of the Old Testament and you encounter stories about what was done in the past by the person's spiritual forefathers. These days we barely know our relatives, much less what they believed and how they lived their lives in light of God's Word and calling. The result is that each generation feels as if it is reinventing Christianity—and a lot of spiritual wisdom and truth gets lost in the process.

What kinds of bridges do you build from your present to the past? Do you stand on the shoulders of the spiritual giants who preceded us to reach a new level of spiritual strength?

Lean on God—Heavily

In the end, one of the greatest lessons you can learn is that raising spiritual champions is beyond your capabilities—but not beyond your personal responsibility. As the world's wisest man noted for our benefit:

> Trust in the LORD with all your heart; do not depend on your own understanding. Seek his will in all you do, and he will direct your paths (Prov. 3:5-6, *NLT*).

Some of the wisest counsel we heard from parents concerned the importance of a regular diet of prayer relating to the challenges of raising spiritual champions, studying the Bible with regard to parenting responsibilities and seeking the encouragement and advice of mature Christians who have been down this road before and have discovered helpful lessons that they are willing to impart. That raises some rather personal questions. How continual and intense is your dialogue with God regarding your parenting practices and experiences? How focused are you upon knowing God's written principles as they relate to your parenting efforts? Who are your closest and most dependable spiritual advisers; and how often do you turn to them for parenting wisdom?

THE SUPPORT OF THE CHURCH

In this chapter, we addressed more of the "how to" than the "what stuff" issues. Remember that we previously discussed what children need in order to rise above the noise of the culture and become spiritual champions (see chapter 4). The content of their needs relates to developing a biblical worldview, knowing themselves and God well enough to discern their mission and vision, achieving genuine security in their relationship with God (both eternal and present-day security), attaining a sense of empowerment to carry out His will regardless of the consequences, developing the supportive relationships that produce both encouragement and accountability and being competent in living out the six pillars of a truly spiritual life (i.e., worship, evangelism, discipleship, stewardship, service and spiritual community).

Spiritual development is not so much about what your children know but who they are.

Spiritual development is not so much about what your children know but who they are. Helping them to become people of godly character starts with you; it is not the job of a church to produce such people.

During the past several years, some high-profile public officials have made a big deal out of the notion that raising a child "takes a village." That is not true. It does not take a village, whether that village is a tribal unit, a religious congregation or a kibbutz. It takes a family that is committed to loving and nurturing children as God intended. Scripture does not call us to put the responsibility for raising children on the community. That obligation is one which parents tacitly accept when they choose to have children. They are not forced to have children. Along with their choice of bearing infants comes the lifelong responsibility to raise them in ways that honor the creator who enabled them to live and to give life to children.

It is true, though, that a family can benefit from the help of a supportive community, especially when that community is grounded in the

Christian faith—a faith that is genuine, unchanging, readily accessible, focused on what matters to God and based on love and truth. Imagine the power that would be available to a family—any and every family—in which the parents are godly, biblically literate, responsible advocates of God's ways and supported by a godly, Bible-driven body of Christians who share the same spiritual goals for every believer's children.

In the next chapter, let's examine how a church can be most effective in aiding parents in fulfilling their God-given responsibility to raise spiritual champions.

CHAPTER 6

HOW CHURCHES HELP TO RAISE SPIRITUAL CHAMPIONS

One of the most exciting aspects of the research we have conducted regarding ministry to children concerns the way in which various churches across the nation work with families in this process. In this chapter, we will explore the investment such churches make in children and their families. My hope is that if you are a parent, you will better understand what a healthy relationship with a church looks like and what you might reasonably expect your church to provide as you raise your children. If you are involved in a church's ministry to children, this chapter will describe the contours of an effective ministry and serve as a checklist against which you might evaluate how well your church's outreach to children is configured.

Conducting this research proved to be more difficult than expected for the following reasons: (1) virtually every church has a children's ministry; (2) families are a crucial segment of the population base for most churches; and (3) almost every congregation asserts that ministry to young people is an important aspect of its mission. However, when we examined what a church does and how it evaluates the efficacy of its work, we found that most churches simply go through the motions. The people involved—usually a handful of the parents whose children are in the program—certainly believe that the spiritual nurturing of children is important, but the activities implemented tend to be ritualistic and of questionable quality; and the outcomes usually are not measured, tracked or interpreted. It also seemed as if a church starts its ministry full of high hopes and energy, committed to high-impact ministry; but as it develops its own persona and ministry niche within the community, the ministry to children generally takes a backseat to the more visible and adult-oriented efforts of the church. Within a decade of holding its first public service, the average church relegates children's ministry to holding-tank status, seeking to keep parents happy, kids occupied, denominational executives satisfied and the church's reputation (i.e., that it offers adequate service in all of the fundamental areas of ministry) intact.

My investigation into churches that help to produce spiritually mature children (i.e., those who know what they believe and why, whose values reflect biblical principles and whose moral and religious activity is indicative of lives that revolve around the faith dimension) has shown that there are five categories of activity that distinguish them from the typical church. Those categories concern perspectives on the spiritual development of and ministry to children, the investment made in such ministry, methods that facilitate the desired outcomes, the content provided through the ministry and the type of workers recruited and released for impactful service among children. Let's delve into these areas.[1]

PERSPECTIVES ON MINISTRY TO CHILDREN

The Underlying Philosophy

Having spent a quarter-century studying various organizations—churches, government agencies, businesses, schools and nonprofit entities—I have found that a few common components surface among those that are effective. One of the typical building blocks is a clear conceptual foundation—a philosophy that permeates every department, program and policy. Not surprisingly, this was true of the best children's ministries, too.

These ministries have clarified the basics of what they stand for and what they exist to produce. There are definitions of what education, Christian discipleship (or "spiritual formation" or whatever term is in vogue at the time the document is crafted) and spiritual maturity mean. Included within those definitions are statements regarding the appropriate roles of key players: parents, teachers, pastors and church staff, mentors, program directors, and so forth.

These documents generally incorporate other key components in the developmental strategy. It was fairly common to read about the expected interaction among biblical truth principles, personal relationships, human reason, authority, experiential learning, traditions, current cultural perspectives, individual values and church doctrine.

In their entirety, these descriptions served as parameters designed to encourage and foster a single product—life transformation. Ultimately, the determinant of effectiveness is whether the person's life has been significantly changed as a result of the spiritual growth that has occurred. These churches often make a critical distinction, though, between change and transformation. Change is a shift that may or may not last, tends to happen at a discrete and identifiable moment in time and is often incremental in nature—almost imperceptible in many cases. Transformation, however, is an enduring process in which the person is radically reformed and does not revert to his or her previous condition.

This distinction is monumental, because transformation is Spirit driven while change is program driven. Transformation is facilitated but unpredictable, and change is caused and inevitable under the right conditions and stimuli. The most effective churches recognize that the goal is to facilitate transformation, yet they understand that they cannot engineer it no matter how sincere, professional, comprehensive and biblical their approach may be. Only God brings about lasting transformation in a person's life. A ministry may have the privilege of enabling such new life to emerge, but it can neither take credit for it nor describe the step-by-step approach that makes it happen. Consequently, the philosophy of children's ministry in these churches tends to express their awe at the miracle of transformation, which is the Church's hope but God's domain.

It is important to note that the statements of philosophy we examined varied from exhaustive to brief. The common trait, however, was that everyone involved in the process of ministering to children had been exposed to and bought into the fundamental aspects of the philosophy, producing a ministry that was internally consistent.

Perceptions of Family

One of the key elements of that ministry philosophy is the acknowledgment that the spiritual development of children is first and foremost the responsibility of parents and that a church is best poised to assist rather than lead in that process. Drawing on biblical principles and precedent, these churches see themselves as serving families by providing emotional, spiritual and material support to parents as they invest in the faith of their children. In other words, the role of the church is to equip and reinforce rather than lead in this dimension. As the director of children's ministry of one congregation put it, "Our goal is to become the greatest friend and best support a parent has ever had."

To pull this off, a church has to work closely with parents. The church must know what parents are seeking to accomplish in the lives of their kids as well as some of the struggles they are encountering in their efforts. The church then tries to figure out how to add value to the process that is already in motion. There is no sense of competition for supremacy, arrogance regarding relative professionalism or a battle to gain the favor of the children. The church offers efforts that reflect its sensitivity to its role—assisting parents. Consequently, the resources used by the church in its ministry to young people are designed to prepare parents for greater effectiveness, to advance existing efforts by the parents, to serve as a catalyst for new developmental ventures attempted by the family and to enhance the quality of the approaches and exercises used to mature children's faith.

The beauty of this process is that when it is working well you cannot tell who is really leading—the church or the parents. There is such a symbiotic relationship between the two that their progress seems carefully coordinated—which, of course, it often is. The result is a powerful two-fisted punch that has a synergistic impact on the children.

The Benefits of Following an Integrated Plan

A dominant reason for the successful interaction with families is that faith development is integrated on several levels. First, the effort to nurture the faith of children is understood by and coordinated among all church staff, lay leaders, teachers and parents. Second, that effort is incorporated into all of the church's programs and events, from the worship services and Sunday School classes to midweek programs and special events. Third, all of this energy is directed toward creating a continual process designed to affect the whole person, facilitate a lifelong journey and transcend barriers associated with age or capacity.

One of the simplest but most profound strategies to foster this integration is for the entire congregation to focus upon the same biblical principle during a particular week. Whether you attend a worship service, youth-group meeting, small-group meeting, prayer service, men's breakfast or elders meeting, the same principle is focused upon during that week. The value of this consistency of focus is that it ensures that everyone in the church is moving in the same direction spiritually, that parents have acquired some core level of knowledge and insight related to the principle (and thus have the ability to converse with and challenge their children on the subject matter during the week) and that a refined body of spiritual wisdom is delivered to congregants within a compact period of time. (We found that these churches rotate the spiritual principles they cover on anywhere from a one-year to a five-year cycle. The duration of the cycle depends upon the instructional strategy utilized by the church.)

Reasonable Expectations

Effectiveness demands a reasonable understanding of what it takes to enable spiritual maturity to occur. The prevailing perspective we discovered among effective ministries is that transformation is a deep work of the Spirit and therefore may take a lot of time. You cannot rush spiritual development; it is a radical reconstruction process slowed down by cultural resistance and personal distractedness. Replacing bad habits with good ones and substituting biblical theology for cultural lore will not happen overnight, even among those who are intensely committed to such transition.

One of the most startling revelations I encountered on this journey was finding that many of the effective ministries have a long-term plan—in some cases an 18-year developmental plan with specific ideals outlined for each age group from infants through high school seniors. While those churches allow for spontaneity and flexibility despite their long-range planning, they are fully committed to implementing their "big picture" plan.

Such a perspective eliminates the "overnight success" mentality and enables the ministry to dig in for the long haul. Whereas most churches develop educational objectives for a year, the most effective ministries identify their goals for a particular year or age group, but those goals are always viewed within the context of a lifelong maturation process.

The Necessity of Starting Young

Physicians assert that children begin to absorb values as early as two years of age. The highly effective ministries, therefore, start their most serious partnership with parents soon thereafter. The plans that most of these churches implement initiate focused developmental activities with children at the age of four or five.

The ways in which this development takes place encompass the choice of songs that are sung in Christian education classes, the nature of the stories told (they are designed to relate to specific principles that fit into the long-term process), the particular curriculum purchased, the vocabulary used by teachers, the games played (they have a spiritual purpose beyond being fun or entertaining) and the crafts undertaken (always related to the spiritual purpose of the meeting).

Starting the developmental process when children are young is a reflection of the underlying philosophy: Because this is part of a spiritual battle, the longer you wait to pursue influence, the more difficult it is to counteract the influence of other parties that have been imprinting their values upon children. At the risk of sounding simplistic, this is an adaptation of the early-bird-gets-the-worm philosophy.

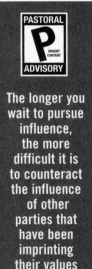

The longer you wait to pursue influence, the more difficult it is to counteract the influence of other parties that have been imprinting their values upon children.

Definitions of Success

Most churches have very simple but ultimately debilitating descriptions of success: growing numbers of students enrolled, consistent attendance, completion of the curriculum in the allotted time, parental satisfaction, minimal discipline problems, and the like. The effective churches have a handful of very different indicators of success. The identity of those descriptions is crucial, because in any organization you get what you value and measure.

Standard number one is experiencing the widespread involvement of the parents in the spiritual development of the children. While that need is satisfied in different ways by various ministries, the effort to nurture children is deemed deficient if it is not led by the parents themselves, in close partnership with the church.

A second indicator of success is that the church is strategically equipping parents to help children develop spiritually. It is for this reason that many of these churches have changed the title of the ministry from "Children's Ministry" to "Family Ministry." They must serve both parents and kids in order to be effective. The equipping process itself entails many elements: increasing parental confidence in their ability to raise spiritual champions, providing practical tools, enhancing the spiritual health of the parents, and so on.

A third cornerstone of success is witnessing elements of transformation in children's lives—not the mere recitation of facts, but lifestyle transitions that suggest a deeper renovation of the heart and spirit. Effective churches are eager to see growth in all dimensions of spirituality—breadth and depth of biblical knowledge, voluntary participation in acts of service, involvement in a genuine spiritual community, daily engagement in worship, and so on—as evidence that children are growing in Christlikeness. They refuse to settle for an imbalanced or one-dimensional standard of efficacy.

CHURCH INVESTMENT IN MINISTRY TO CHILDREN

Prayer, Prayer and More Prayer

Measuring the impact of prayer is a curious challenge. On the one hand, it is like striving to catch the wind—you just cannot get your arms around it and control it. On the other hand, assessing the difference that prayer makes may be a simple act of observation and faith. In my judgment, the prayer investment made by the effective churches may be the single most important venture of their ministries.

I found that the most productive children's ministries have five streams of prayer offered to God. The first of those is from the teachers of the youngsters. As a matter of course, teachers are encouraged to pray for each student on a regular basis. They are encouraged to pray as specifically as possible, identifying the deeper needs of each student as they become evident during the times of teaching and ministry.

Second, we saw that the teachers pray as a team, usually on a weekly basis, along with other staff and the church leaders associated with the ministry to children. The intent is to ask for God's blessings and guidance related to particular needs and situations, building a deeper esprit de corps through the act of entering God's presence in unity. My sense was that these prayer times also contributed to the sense that those engaging the children were on the front lines of the spiritual battle and were reliant upon God's power and authority to build up children in their faith.

A third prayer component is the involvement of intercessors who volunteer to faithfully pray for the teachers and students. These individuals tend to have regular contact with the teachers—at least once a week—to gain updated information about needs, concerns, victories and goals regarding the students, the classes and the teachers. In some cases, the teachers would join the intercessors in prayer, but more often the outsiders mount a silent but effective vigil on behalf of those working face-to-face with the congregation's children. The reminders to the teachers that they are not alone in the battle—conveyed through telephone calls, e-mails, postcards and other forms of personal contact—seem both to lift the spirits of the teachers and to renew their commitment to helping the young people grow spiritually. Without any statistics to back this up, I would also conclude that the "prayer cover" these spiritual warriors receive is one of the most significant elements in their willingness to continue to fight the good fight through their ministry to children.

Fourth, because the ministry to children is highly valued in these churches, it is not surprising to find that the entire congregation frequently prays for that ministry. The senior pastor as well as other church leaders would direct the congregation to unite in prayer during worship services, Sunday School classes, midweek events, congregational meetings and leadership meetings, asking God to honor the church's efforts to grow children who would become pleasing and capable servants. Perhaps the most impressive realities of such prayer are the regularity of those requests made to God as well as the apparent sincerity of the importance of those requests. In other words, these congregations do not give lip service to praying for the children, so they can satisfy their spiritual duty and scratch another item off their to-do list. The prayers for the children and those working with them seem to be intense and authentic.

The fifth avenue of prayer emanates from the parents. Some of these churches organize prayer times for parents. Others have forums for parental support during which prayer is a featured activity. There are some ministries that have prayer letters for parents to include the needs of their children or child-rearing efforts, and others that have elders and other prayer partners specifically assigned to pray for parent-child requests.

If you believe that prayers are answered by God and that the spiritual development of children matters, then it makes sense to have a genuine and significant prayer effort aimed at seeking God's blessing on this aspect of ministry. These churches are unusually effective, I believe, because they constantly beg God to bless the work related to the moral and spiritual maturation of their congregation's young people. This is not something done in a formulaic manner, nor is it undertaken as a dry routine. Prayer works in these churches because the body of believers shares God's heartbeat about the importance of children and believes that prayer makes a difference in people's lives. The result is obvious: God blesses their efforts.

The Chief Advocate

Senior pastors have a very challenging job. They are charged with maximizing the aggregate spiritual health of the church God has given them to lead. The numerous well-intentioned congregants who try to persuade the pastor to prioritize a particular ministry complicate the pastor's efforts. Maintaining a sense of vision and God's priorities while keeping everyone focused and involved is difficult.

Invariably, the churches where the children's ministry prospers are those led by pastors who are unapologetic advocates for that ministry focus. These leaders demonstrate their support for the children's ministry in various ways. They represent its best interests in strategic meetings, such as when budgets and staffing decisions are made. They teach the congregation about the importance of children and motivate parents to take their responsibilities seriously. They keep an eye on the quality of the church activities offered for the spiritual nourishment of children. They celebrate the victories and progress achieved by the children's ministry, communicating those outcomes in sermons, presentations and written communications to the congregants. They encourage adults to get involved by working with the kids, using their talents and spiritual gifts in ways that advance the development of the young people.

Because a senior pastor can only be a strong advocate of a very few ministries, he or she must choose those that are both strategic and influential while fitting within the boundaries of the unique vision God has provided for that church. As a personal observation, I believe that if the pastor does not include the ministry to children as one of the top church priorities, the chance of that ministry reaching its potential and having a significant impact on the lives of the church's children is severely reduced.

A Learner's Mentality

One of the most endearing qualities of the effective children's ministries is that the youth workers are eager to learn how to do their best when working with children. To maximize their capacity, they read publications that challenge and stimulate their thinking, they visit other churches that are effective to learn new approaches or identify gaps in their own philosophy, they interview new members of the church to glean ideas from the past experiences of those families, and they develop a network of like-minded ministries with which they can share ideas and experiences toward pushing the boundaries. There is no sense of territorialism about what they discover. These churches freely share their insights based on the perspective that what they have discovered is insight from God designed for the Church at-large and the expectation that they will benefit from the ministry insights shared by other churches that have moved forward.

METHODS AND TECHNIQUES THAT FACILITATE IMPACT

Specific Goal Setting

Churches with successful children's ministries have discovered that it is not enough to have a comprehensive, transformation-driven philosophy of ministry. They believe that having specific goals is important, too. Sometimes these churches come under fire from other churches for "boxing in the Holy Spirit." Their response to such criticism is that their goals are built upon the vision and direction they have received from God and that they are always open to redirection since the actual transformation process is spearheaded and accomplished by the Holy Spirit—in conjunction with the church's work. Further, because transformation is not easy to assess, they try to identify the steps to such personal reformation and look for evidence of progress toward that large-scale outcome.

In examining the goals and the process that lead to that outcome, it appeared that these churches made every reasonable attempt to engage each student's mind, heart and spirit. This meant offering intellectually stretching experiences, emotionally striking challenges and spiritually moving interactions. The goals of the ministry thus touched on all three of these bases. Intellectual goals encompassed age-appropriate outcomes related to Scripture memorization, biblical interpretation, contextual analysis, skill at connecting faith and social conditions, effective verbal communication of one's beliefs in a clear and nonoffensive manner, critical analysis of worldview communications, and so forth. Among the emotional outcomes for which goals were crafted were instances of verbal encouragement, demonstrations of compassionate stewardship, empathy toward those in difficult circumstances, passion for reaching unsaved people, genuine love of God, gratitude for His grace, awe at His majestic nature, and so on. Spiritual outcomes included inspired and frequent prayer, prayer that transcends response to personal needs, heartfelt worship, self-initiated evangelism, acts of service to the poor and disadvantaged, voluntary accountability, and the like.

One of the most impressive observations related to such churches is that they designed their goals in relation to developmental theory. In other words, they are aware of what a child of a particular age is able to handle in terms of concepts, language, experiences and relationships. A child who is 5 has a different concept of the Holy Spirit than a child of 12—and no amount of storytelling, language sensitivity and Bible memorization will alter his or her ability to grasp such an abstract concept at that young age. Consequently, not only is classroom content built around such an understanding of age-based development, but also the goals set by the church reflect reasonable expectations for each grade level. (We'll dive into the topic of evaluation more deeply in the next chapter.)

Balanced Activity

Among the many factors that seem to produce positive spiritual growth in young people is ensuring that they are able to relate to the material in ways that make sense to them. In that regard, the effective ministries tend to provide three important elements.

First, effective ministries convey important information and lessons in ways that the student relates to. As noted earlier, some learn through a visual presentation (i.e., videos, pictures, reading) while others have to hear the information in order to process it, and still others must experience the lesson through a kind of trial-and-error, multisensory adventure. Although it is resource depleting and demands extra effort by the adults involved, there is a growing contingency of churches that are intentionally providing multiple means of conveying spiritual lessons to their children to ensure that each youngster has a genuine opportunity to grasp the material being covered.

A second insight is that these ministries are keenly responsive to the adult-child ratio in their activities. The upper limit deemed acceptable by these churches is five elementary school students to each adult involved. Some of the churches insisted on ratios as low as 3 to 1. (Among junior high school students, the ratio was allowed to balloon to 10 to 1 in many of these churches.) The importance of sustaining low ratios was to facilitate each child's having a greater degree of personal attention. These churches want every child to feel known, loved and significant and to have any obstacles to growth quickly identified and overcome.

The third clue to the success of these churches is that they balance activities done in small groups with those done in a large-group setting. To have impact, some efforts require the intimacy and personal attention that a small-group experience offers; other inputs can be more effectively accomplished through a large-group experience.

Mentors Who Stay in Touch

Building on the balance factors mentioned above, another key technique effective ministries employ is motivating their youth workers to build genuine relationships with the children. These churches encourage the parents and staff to spend time playing with the kids as a means to giving the youngsters a good experience while enabling the adults to gain insight into the needs and spiritual condition of the children. Through conversation and forms of entertaining interaction, the adults can assess the needs of the children while developing a deeper level of trust with them. The conversations that ensue provide important clues regarding the language the children will understand, the issues they grapple with, their personal needs, how they process information and the growth that they have made since the relationship was initiated. The desired ancillary benefit for the youth workers is also significant—to enjoy being with the children!

Depth Rather Than Breadth

I found that most of these ministries share an unusual technique: They identify a number of core principles that they hope to convey to children and they return to those principles year after year. Naturally, they approach those principles differently each year, taking into account the developmental capacity of the child, but the goal is to enable each child to master the content and personal applications of each principle in an age-appropriate way each year.

This can be a tricky process. We have found, for instance, that many churches repeat the same lessons over and over. The typical church focuses on a selection of the following Bible stories with its children:

Widely Taught Bible Story	Place in the Bible
Creation	Genesis 1—2
Adam and Eve	Genesis 2—5
Noah and the flood	Genesis 6—11
Joseph and his family	Gen. 37—50
Moses and the plagues	Exodus 5—11
Moses parts the Red Sea	Exodus 13—15

Moses and the Ten Commandments	Exodus 19—24
Joshua enters the Promised Land	Joshua 1—12
Saul becomes Israel's first king	1 Samuel 8—12
David slays Goliath	1 Samuel 17
David and Bathsheba	2 Samuel 11—12
Solomon asks God for wisdom	2 Chronicles 1
Esther saves the Jews	Esther 5—8
Job's faith is tested	Job 1—2
Daniel interprets the king's dream	Daniel 2
Shadrach, Meshach and Abednego survive the furnace	Daniel 3
Daniel survives the lions' den	Daniel 6
Jonah and the whale	Jonah 1—2
The virgin birth of Jesus Christ	Matthew 1—2
Satan tempts Jesus	Matthew 4
The Sermon on the Mount	Matthew 5—7
Jesus multiplies the fish and loaves of bread	Matthew 14
The Last Supper	Matthew 26
Jesus' arrest and crucifixion	Matthew 26—27
Jesus' resurrection	Matthew 28
The Great Commission	Matthew 28
Jesus turns water into wine at Cana	John 2
The Holy Spirit arrives (Pentecost)	Acts 2
Paul is converted to Christianity	Acts 9—10
The spiritual gifts	1 Corinthians 12
The nature of love	1 Corinthians 13
Faith without works is dead	James 2

A typical children's ministry will touch upon 20 to 40 specific Bible episodes in a given year. As a child ages and works his or her way through the program, the classes return to most of those stories but without significantly varying the presentation angle or the point of the story.

An unfortunate result of this repetitiveness is that teachers lose their freshness and send a message to students that the Bible has a limited array of lessons to convey. We found that students are likely to feel that they are not learning anything new, leading to the impression that they already know everything of value there is to know about the Christian faith. (That is, in fact, the belief of three-quarters of all churchgoing adolescents—and raises unfortunate implications for those young people.)

We also learned that while many churches feel vindicated in their approach by the fact that many of their children can identify the basic contours of the stories and can describe some details related to the key characters, the young people are clueless regarding the fundamental principles and lessons to be drawn from those narratives.

The effective churches, however, delve deeper each year with new insights and personal applications related to each principle, building upon the lessons offered in prior years rather than simply repeating those lessons in different words. Rather than repeat the same stories in the same context, they focus on the principles to be gleaned and consider each of those stories from a new angle or within a different instructional context.

Parents' Involvement

Effective ministries insist on the regular participation of parents. Beyond asserting that the parents take the lead role in the spiritual nurturing of their children, these churches have regulations regarding the involvement of parents in the children's ministry, expecting them to invest a minimum number of days or hours in the programs, based upon their skills and gifts. They also request that parents attend several class sessions or special events with their children each year, which deepens the connection between what the church and the parents are doing in raising spiritual champions.

Effective ministries insist on the regular participation of parents.

Like many churches, these ministries ask children to bring home evidence of what they are doing at church, but they also provide materials that help parents throughout the week to build on the seeds planted by the church during the weekend.

Surprisingly, a number of the effective churches even set up parent-teacher conferences to formalize the dialogue between home and church, to identify observed obstacles to spiritual growth and to clarify forthcoming lessons to which the children will be exposed. Among the many benefits of the contact between the teachers and parents is the deepening of the relationship between the ministry and home, while the formality of a student review process reflects the importance of the children's spiritual development.

Content That Brings About Change

Curriculum Selection

There are several dozen companies that produce high-quality curriculum for church use. Thousands of churches purchase those resources. However, we found that most of the effective children's ministries do not use any form of standardized curriculum; instead, they develop their own. A major reason for this approach is that these churches have a long-term, worldview-oriented approach to spiritual development that is not reflected in the standardized products available. Even though it takes more time, expertise and resources, these churches write and design their own materials each year. They may borrow ideas and concepts from the standardized resources, but they create a full line of curriculum to meet their unique needs.

I was surprised that these churches generally revise the curriculum each year—even most professional curriculum publishers do not engage in such extensive rewrites on such a regular basis. The main reason for such an investment, it turns out, is to ensure that the children's materials are integrated into the aggregate ministry focus of the church, allowing parents to maximize their involvement in the developmental process. The in-house approach also enables the church to make stronger ties between biblical principles and current world events, enhancing the perceived relevance of biblical principles. What the self-published materials lack in artistic design they make up for in substantive consistency and real-time relevance.

Character and Worldview Emphasis

The lessons developed focus less on story lines and memorizing content than on the central principles of a story and the personal applications of those principles. Effective churches tend to emphasize the values and perspectives that build individual character. The cumulative impact of those values lead children to the brink of possessing a biblical worldview, which is the ultimate objective of most of these churches. The discussions fostered by the materials address moral choices, central beliefs and how one's beliefs lead to appropriate lifestyle choices.

The intentional development of a biblical worldview requires years of integrated effort. Each year a child is in the program, the core principles are probed more deeply and the child is pushed to identify personal applications. Teachers emphasize the connection between all of the scriptural principles addressed, which helps the child see how a worldview based on those principles is constructed. With each passing lesson, the church strives to add a measure of accountability to the process, enforcing the significance of those principles.

Personal Involvement in Ministry

A standard expectation in these effective churches is that every child should be personally involved in some form of ministry. "Kids get in a frame of mind that you go to church to receive, but they never get the message that to whom much is given, much is expected," explained one of the ministry directors we interviewed. "We believe it is imperative to instill the value that a Christian is blessed to pass that blessing on to others, and that can only be accomplished if the person is actively serving other people."

The act of serving other people is cultivated from the earliest years these children engage in the church's program. Whether those forms of service are simple—visiting people in nursing homes, making birthday cards to send to sick people, earnestly praying for specific individuals or doing a work project at the church—or more substantial, the hope is to build a habit. Often, the church uses these experiences to assist kids in determining their spiritual gifts and seeing ways in which they can apply those gifts for the benefit of others.

Family Service Projects

In addition to the personal service expectation, many of the effective churches try to reinforce the importance of outreach efforts by setting up opportunities for families to work together in serving needy people. Many of these churches have discovered that once parents recognize their obligation to direct the spiritual development of their children and then recognize how integral serving others is in that journey, they are open to serving alongside their youngsters in meaningful projects. However, they often have no idea how to put those desires into action. Consequently, the church sets up projects for families, serving as a kind of administrative assistant to the family.

Teachers and coaches often use these family service experiences as points of departure for class discussions, examples for their teaching or the subject of assignments. The more all of the threads of the children's growth experiences are tied together, the stronger the imprint that will be left on their heart.

PEOPLE WHO MAKE IT HAPPEN

Recruiting Strategically

Most of the churches we have studied indicate that recruiting quality workers for the children's ministry is a hardship. The effective churches have a very different experience. Deeper inspection revealed that this difference is primarily due to a divergent recruiting strategy.

The highly effective ministries begin by making sure every potential lay worker understands the expectations up front. Initially, this is achieved by providing potential helpers with clear job descriptions. These churches want to ensure that there are as few surprises as possible when someone signs up to minister to children. The outline of each position details the amount of time expected to be invested, the skills that will be most useful in the position and key elements of the ministry philosophy that must be adopted to fit in. It is hoped that the workers will know the nature of the commitment demanded so that when they sign on, they know what they are getting themselves into and the church can count on them to deliver what they promise.

Perhaps unexpectedly, we find that these churches say they only want people who feel called to work with children to be involved in that ministry. Some clergy have responded that if they took that tack in their congregation, they'd never be able to recruit enough people to fill the classrooms. The reply from the effective churches, however, is that they trust God to provide them with the resources they need to get every worthwhile job completed—and that they generally have no problems meeting the demand for workers.

A critical dimension of their success also lies in the commitment to prayer. The church's leaders regularly pray not only for the children's growth and the strength of the program but also that God would motivate the appropriate people to come forward and enlist in the children's ministry. Even when things are running smoothly, you will find the pastor, staff and elders praying for the continued provision of qualified teachers, assistants, coaches and prayer partners, and for parents to work intimately with the church's representatives. Once again, the deep commitment to prayer clearly makes a significant difference.

Workers are also easier to come by in these churches because they get the training they need—before they oblige themselves to a position. Some observers have noted that this seems inefficient, but the effective churches respond that it enables a potential youth worker to understand the skills, expectations and ministry style before making any serious commitments. This substantially reduces the worker dropout rate.

Improving the Role of Clergy and Staff

In most churches with ministry staff besides the senior pastor, the role of each staff member is to lead one or more ministry programs or departments. In the churches that have effective ministries to children, the assignment to staffers is quite different: Empower the laity to lead the ministry forward, and dedicate your time and resources to supporting their ministry efforts.

In these congregations, the staff member associated with the children's ministry strives to be available and accessible to assist parents and other adults as the youth worker ministers to children. The objective is simple: Make sure that the youth workers have what they need when they need it and that they are able to do what they need to do when they need to do it. The staff member aggressively seeks opportunities to supply ideas, tangible resources (e.g., sharpened pencils, markers for the white board, curriculum, construction paper, and so on), facilities and equipment and encouragement—whatever it takes to make the youth workers shine.

Incorporating Team-Based Leadership

Many ministries falter because their success hinges on the tireless and wise efforts of a single volunteer or staff person. Such a structure invites disaster. If that indispensable individual is ill, absent, quits, burns out, reaches his or her level of incompetence or simply becomes overwhelmed by the weight of the responsibilities involved, then the entire program suffers.

Effective ministries develop great team leadership.[2] This transcends merely having teams of volunteers working in unison. Team leadership is based on having a small group of true leaders, probably no more than four or five, who have complementary leadership skills, blending their talents in cooperation as they strive to enable the ministry to achieve the vision God has given to it. Because each of these leaders fulfills a different function within the aggregate leading of the ministry, none of them becomes overburdened or indispensable. Instead, each contributes what he or she enjoys and is best at doing. The quality of the decisions made by teams is almost always superior to that delivered by a single leader trying to cover all the bases. While team-based leadership provides a victory for everyone involved, the biggest winners are the children.

Training the Staff

Nearly every church with a children's ministry claims to offer some type of training for its youth workers. As you might expect, the training provided by the most effective ministries has some unique characteristics.

First, the effective churches do less training than the average church. That surprises many observers, but the underlying reason is that the church does not want to overdo it. Most of the individuals involved in children's ministry are parents or grandparents—that is, people who understand kids pretty well. The training they need is minimal and can be accomplished fairly quickly if it is well presented and intelligently developed. A lot of the training provided by effective churches relates less to understanding children and families and more to how the church's ministry integrates the material into a larger frame of reference (e.g., your church's vision, a biblical worldview or a 15-year educational process). After the introductory training session for new helpers has been completed, many of the effective ministries offer further training sessions just two or three times a year.

Second, the training is high quality. "My primary goal," explained one director of children's ministries, "is to be certain that I never insult my workers and always use their time well. To do that, I have to know each of them and what they're doing and tailor the training to their needs." I have yet to witness at an effective church a "kitchen sink" training session (i.e., a session that tries to cover broad principles that are indisputable but generally too vague to be of much value to any individual). The great churches often provide their training according to grade level so that teachers, mentors and assistants have a customized presentation that relates specifically to their experience and needs. Training sessions that bring together all the youth workers at the same time are unusual. "If I don't respect these people's time and talents," noted another ministry leader, "I won't have them long—if they're worth having at all."

Finally, it appears that training makes its mark in these churches because the ministry spends the money required to get experts to deliver the goods. It is commonplace for these churches to have instructors from parachurch ministries, educational institutes, seminaries and universities, medical clinics and other churches rather than relying upon one or more staff members who may have the responsibility but lack the expertise to get youth workers to the next level of performance. Here again is a reflection of the church's view of ministry to children: They spend money on premium trainers because they believe that what goes into the life of a child reaps multiplied rewards for many years to come. There is no perceived value to using shortcuts or saving money when investing in the spiritual development of their children.

Protecting the Children

Many states now have laws that mandate the kind of background checks that must be done before someone is certified to work in a classroom with children. However, I learned that most of the effective churches have security procedures that go far beyond what state regulations require—and many had those self-imposed requirements in place long before state agencies handed down their rulings.

The reason for this careful approach is that churches want to accomplish four things. First, they want to ensure that every child is safe. These young ones are precious and vulnerable; therefore, making sure that they are in a secure setting with loving people is paramount. Second, each of these churches want to communicate a critical message to parents: "We will do our best to love and protect your children as if they were our own." It is a bond of trust that allows parents to hand over their children to a church, even for an hour or two. Deepening that trust is important if the church is to have the privilege of working with the family to deepen the children's spiritual moorings over the course of time. Third, loving young people reflects the importance that these churches assign to the spiritual development of kids. It is one thing to make that claim; it is another to go through the painstaking, resource-depleting activity of doing things like security checks and testing of youth-worker applicants. Finally, these churches wish to demonstrate to the government that it will comply with every reasonable request made by its agencies. Indisputably, looking out for the best interests of children is one of those areas in which the church and government share a common interest.

Reinforcing the Youth Workers

Earlier in this chapter it was mentioned that it is relatively easy for the most effective churches to recruit and retain their adult helpers. One of the major reasons for that ability is that these churches are intentional about making their workers feel valuable. If these people are worth anything, then their time and talents are valuable and could be used in other venues, probably to greater monetary profit. Therefore, the effective churches do not take their volunteers for granted; instead, they consistently communicate the value those helpers are providing and the long-term benefits they are instilling in the lives of their young charges.

Upon watching how these ministries operate, several specific practices seem to occur over and over among these churches. For instance, they listen attentively to what their youth workers are saying. The idea is not to placate them or make them feel as if they were heard but to genuinely consider the experiences and concerns of each worker and respond in a meaningful manner. The youth workers know they are heard because their words generate a thoughtful response from the church—whether the response is facilitated by the pastor, staff, lay leaders or fellow youth workers.

Another example is the regular heartfelt demonstrations of appreciation given to those who spend their time working with children. Such incidents of gratitude come in different forms: the pastor sitting in on a class for 5 or 10 minutes, strictly as an observer, and then sending a handwritten postcard or letter thanking each youth worker personally for his or her help and mentioning something specific that had taken place during the class that was exemplary; private dinners at the pastor's home with a handful of youth workers; testimonials given of each youth worker's efforts during the worship services or congregational meetings; articles posted in the church newsletter about the youth workers and their experiences with the children; or books purchased for the youth workers that relate to the particular struggles or topics germane to their current endeavors with the children.

A final example of showing appreciation to those who minister to children is allowing them a chance to share their insights and dreams with larger groups of adults. Some of these churches invite youth workers to speak to the congregation during a worship service once a month or so; others have them share in Sunday School classes or other venues. The objective is to give these adults an outlet for their discoveries while captivating the hearts of the other adults in the church.

Ministries That Go Beyond the Average

As you read these brief descriptions of the efforts made by the most effective children's ministries in the nation, one thing probably becomes clear: These churches are serious about blessing children! They go out of their way to do the unexpected because it is the right thing to do. They incorporate the talents of everyone who has a heart to love and nurture children because that is the role of the Church: to enable people to use their gifts in areas of passion to produce benefits for the kingdom of God—benefits that spill over into the home, the marketplace and the church itself.

I pray that you do not turn to the next chapter feeling that these are "superchurches"—congregations composed of extraordinarily skilled people whose programs are heavily funded showcases that are far removed from your experience and possibilities. These churches are just like yours—except, perhaps, that they have prioritized their ministry to children and refused to settle for anything less than God's best for their lives. They are not all megachurches, although many of them have become large congregations primarily because of the emphasis on and the quality of their children's ministry—how they love and nurture children. And these are not churches that hire the best and the brightest to mastermind their programs. In fact, in a substantial number of these churches, there is no one staff member dedicated to leading the children's ministry.

The role of the Church is to enable people to use their gifts in areas of passion to produce benefits that spill over into the home, the marketplace and the church itself.

More than anything, I have come away convinced that any and every church could have a world-class ministry to children if it so desired. There seem to be three critical factors on the path to effectiveness. The first is leadership. The leaders of the church must possess an authentic passion and a God-given vision for this emphasis and must be willing to fight the tough battles in terms of allocating the church's resources, motivating people's involvement and maintaining a high standard for quality.

A second key component relates to the focus on worldview. Every church would do well to carefully design its ministry to children in such a manner that the ministry continually promotes a biblical worldview. The church need not call it by that name and it need not call much attention to this approach, but providing the church's young people with the information, experiences, skills and encouragement required to steadfastly develop and live in concert with a biblical worldview will facilitate genuine and consistent spiritual growth.

Finally, success in ministering to children is about perseverance. No child becomes holy and righteous after involvement in a church program for a year or two. This is a process that demands parent-church partnership (which in itself requires diligence), a long-term strategy and a process maintained by the church, the view that each child is a Kingdom resource that needs continual and progressive investments for many consecutive years, and the continual involvement and maintenance of gifted and called leaders, teachers, coaches and assistants who will provide continuity and quality over the long haul.

Every church can develop a great ministry to children. But such a result must be intentional.

CHAPTER 7

BETTER PERFORMANCE THROUGH EVALUATION

Imagine that you are the parent of a nine-year-old girl. You recently moved to a new home whose location you chose with great care based primarily upon the high quality and stellar reputation of the schools in that community. You have high hopes for your little girl and want her to get the best education available so that she has as many options as possible at her disposal once she completes her schooling.

The first semester in the new school district seemed to go well. You regularly asked your daughter how she was doing in her schoolwork and consistently heard that things were going well. You were eager to meet her teacher at the end of the semester to find out in greater detail how your child was performing and what specific forms of assistance you could provide to better support your preteen.

Finally, it is time for the long-awaited parent-teacher conference. You get to the classroom and meet the young, bright-eyed instructor. You inquire as to your child's progress. "Oh, she's doing just great," beams the teacher.

"What is her grade-point average so far?" you ask, hoping to get a more definitive sense of just how "great" things are going.

"Oh, we don't actually have any grades. But she's doing very well," comes the confident reply.

"But you must have some test scores to look at." The teacher keeps smiling but shakes her head from side to side, dismissing the idea. "Some evaluations of in-class exercises?" You receive another dissenting shake of the head. "Notes assessing her class participation or math skills?" Wrong again.

"How is it that you know she's doing so well if there are no tests, no papers, no grades, no written evaluations and no apparent measurements of any kind?" you ask, incredulous that four months have passed with seemingly no effort by the instructor to objectively gauge your daughter's progress.

"Oh, well, I can tell that she's doing well," the teacher begins. "You see, she comes to class every day. She almost always has her textbook with her. And it's a very good text; I picked it out myself after comparing more than a dozen different books. I have a sense that she is rather bright and she seems to pay attention most of the time. You should be proud of her—she is polite, she keeps her desk clean and organized, and the other students like her. And believe me," the educator says with her biggest smile yet, "all semester long I have worked very hard to teach the necessary math principles to the best of my ability."

"But how," you persist, "do you know she's learning anything?"

For the first time, the teacher's warm smile turns into a frown. "But I just explained that to you."

If you were that parent, you would be incensed. No tests, reports, essays, practicums or evaluations of any type were used to judge how well—or if—your child was learning the critical skills and lessons. You would raise a fuss, demanding that your child receive the kind of careful measurement process that would reveal whether or not she was being prepared for life.

This same situation is exactly what we face in regard to the most important dimension of our children's lives, yet we shrug off the lack of evaluation by saying spiritual development is an extracurricular pursuit—a value-added component—and that as long as the teachers mean well and try hard, the Bible is the main text, your child seems engaged and there are no significant behavioral difficulties, then the process must be going well.

But how do you *know*?

WHO'S FOOLING WHOM?

Our research reveals that for the most part, we have lulled ourselves into complacency regarding the spiritual growth of our children. That self-satisfaction is enabled solely because we have no objective measures against which to compare our subjective feelings. Take a look at some of our findings:

- Nearly 9 out of every 10 parents of churched kids (87 percent) are satisfied with whatever it is their youngsters are receiving from their church.

- Two-thirds (64 percent) of the nation's Protestant senior pastors claim their church is doing an excellent or good job of helping kids to share their faith in Christ. However, we found that a large portion of churched kids never do so.

- Four-fifths of our senior pastors say their church is doing an excellent or good job of enabling kids to understand and engage in worship. Our studies among kids show that 4 out of every 5 churched 13-year-olds do not know what worship is, and a substantial majority of them admit that they do not feel they have ever experienced God's presence.

- Three-quarters (74 percent) of the pastors interviewed claim their church is doing an excellent or good job of getting kids to adopt a biblical worldview. In spite of that, we know that fewer than 5 percent of churched kids who are born again have a biblical worldview by age 13.

The way that parents evaluate spiritual development appears to be even less demanding. For instance, when we asked parents to identify the "absolutely necessary outcomes" from their child's involvement in a church, there were only three results that at least two-thirds of the parents agreed upon: (1) they want their child to receive more information about God and faith matters; (2) they want their child to be well behaved, and disciplined if necessary; and (3) they personally want to receive some guidance or tips concerning the child's further spiritual development. In other words, parents maintain some rather minimal expectations: (1) teach the kids some of that Bible stuff; (2) make sure they stay out of trouble; and (3) give the parents some encouragement along with a few ideas on how to survive until next week!

Leader after leader of children's ministries verified this perspective. One of those leaders, a children's pastor with 27 years of experience, described it this way:

In my 27 years of ministering to children and their families, I have never once had a parent come up to me and ask how their child is progressing spiritually. Every weekend I get parent after parent chasing me down to ask about their kids. But what they want to know is whether or not their child showed up to class, whether their child had his or her Bible and whether their child was well behaved during the class. Nobody seems to care very much about how the child is doing spiritually, as if merely showing up two or three times a month precludes having to even ask the question.

This corresponds to the previously noted facts demonstrating that because parents have very simplistic notions of what spiritual growth looks like, most parents think they're doing an above-average job of facilitating genuine spiritual growth in their youngsters. Consider the contradictions and implications related to some of the data presented earlier in this book:

- Even though only 5 percent of churched parents have a biblical worldview, two-thirds (64 percent) of all churched parents think they are doing an excellent or good job of helping their children to develop a worldview based on the Bible.

- Although fewer than 10 percent of churched households spend any time at all during a typical week either reading the Bible or engaging in substantive prayer as a family unit, about 3 out of every 4 (72 percent) churched parents believe they are doing well when it comes to providing a regular regimen of spiritual experiences and instruction to their children.

- Despite the fact that fewer than one-twentieth of churched households ever worship God outside of a church service or have any type of regular Bible study or devotional time together during a typical week and that almost two-thirds of the children of churched families are not born again, three-fourths (72 percent) of those parents claim they are doing a stellar job of nurturing their children's relationship with God.

You cannot avoid shaking your head at these figures and wondering how we allow ourselves to set the bar so low. Keep in mind that if children are gleaning anything at all from their church experience, they will return to their home and watch to see if the principles and beliefs taught to them are consistent with and reinforced by the behavior of their primary spiritual nurturers—their parents. Sadly, even when useful information and ideas learned from church experiences are grasped by these children, they are lost or negated in the spiritual confusion that reigns within the typical churched household.

In all of the evaluation research we have conducted during the past two decades, I have seen firsthand that *you get what you measure*. Unfortunately, most parents are pleased simply to have churchgoing children. If the children learn anything of positive value while they are at church, it is deemed a bonus—if it is even noticed. There is usually little if any attempt by the family to track what the child is learning and integrating. The outcomes that are measured more closely relate to behavior modification than to spiritual development.

If we are serious about preparing our children to become spiritual champions—not just church members or Bible owners, but individuals who live every moment of their lives for the cause of Christ and with a determination to be holy because God is holy—then we must incorporate some degree of assessment into the spiritual development processes that we introduce into kids' lives.

IS IT REALLY DISTASTEFUL?

Spiritual evaluation—or any type of evaluation, for that matter—is no easy matter. To conduct meaningful evaluation entails more than just deciding to take a few measurements. To engage in evaluation implies that you have taken the time to identify specific outcomes that are important; and by trying to determine performance levels, you assert that those outcomes are significant enough to invest resources into a measurement process.

Evaluation insinuates something even deeper: You are willing to discover and address the truth of the situation. When there is no defensible evaluation process, assessment is based on assumptions and intuition. Introducing a more telling means of assessment, however, shows that you have the courage to face the facts and to deal with them, whether they are laudable or abysmal. Uncovering the facts indicates that you are committed to making changes merited by the findings. Anything less suggests that you are a hypocrite.

In fact, once you initiate an evaluation process, you are committing yourself to a long-term protocol of assessment. After all, a single measurement in time is interesting and revealing, but it is insufficient. It does not provide the extensive window of insight required to promote true transformation. Realize that once you unleash this process, you are making a commitment to repeat the evaluation over time so that you can honestly track changes, for better or worse, and react accordingly.

WHAT IS A MEANINGFUL EVALUATION?

In chapter 6, we explored what the most effective churches do to help transform children into spiritual champions. Let me note that those congregations help parents raise up spiritual champions through the judicious use of continual evaluations related to how well each child is developing spiritually.

Following a well-established ministry pattern, the churches that offer the most effective outreach to children blaze their own trails when it comes to assessment. There are no standardized tests they all turn to or research firms they hire to conduct on-site profiles of their children. The one component they all share is a sense of urgency about having an objective understanding of what is working and what is not, and whether or not a given child is making discernible strides in his or her spiritual development. That common refusal to substitute good intentions for good outcomes distinguishes those ministries that facilitate spiritual growth from those who only talk about it.

Sometimes we need to "back in" to a viable process, which very well may be the case regarding spiritual evaluation. Perhaps we can start by describing what spiritual maturity is not. Outcomes such as parental satisfaction with their children's progress, the children's happiness with their church experience, frequency of attendance and coming from a "good Christian family" are not necessarily relevant factors.

As often as not, I found that churches attempt to discern a child's spiritual progress through some fairly subjective means. Regular and probing conversations about moral and spiritual matters may provide some initial clues. Seeking indicators of the young person's passion for the ways and approval of God—whether that be through engagement in personal Bible study, journaling, voluntary participation in service projects and missions trips, donating personal funds to ministry efforts or body language unconsciously exhibited during times of worship—add more insight to the ultimate conclusions drawn.

Figuring out if spiritual progress is being made can be determined by looking at more than just overtly religious factors. For instance, many of the youth workers we interviewed noted that they rely on input gained by observing how the child acts in the company of peers, particularly in situations where one's values are on open display (e.g., does he or she join the crowd or does he or she refuse to make fun of another student), gauging the character of a child's close friends, listening to the interaction between a child and his or her siblings and parents, and even studying the types of media purchased and preferred by the youngster (e.g., favorite TV shows and videos, favorite musical CDs and favorite actors, actresses and athletes). Every event in our daily activities provides an opportunity for us to display what's going on inside of us. All it takes is someone who cares to watch, analyze and respond in order to bring about greater spiritual health and maturity.

PASTORAL ADVISORY

Effective ministry to children—by parents or church-related youth workers— demands substantial energy, time and interaction.

All of these rather subjective measures require one irreplaceable element—a relationship with the child that causes the youth worker to care deeply about the child and allows the youth worker to make such observations. Redirecting a young person's energy and inclinations dictates someone caring enough to gather and interpret the raw data.

This is a major reason why youth ministries that are based on large-group events have little lasting impact: Nobody really knows the children, cares about them, follows up on them or personally directs their paths in the way that they should go. Teaching a gymnasium packed with kids may be emotionally satisfying for the teacher, but the process leaves much to be desired in terms of human impact. At its root, effective ministry to children—by parents or church-related youth workers—demands substantial energy, time and interaction. There is no substitute for the personal touch.

How Do I Measure Progress?

What then might a parent or a church-based youth worker do to get a sense of where a child stands in terms of spiritual maturity and whether or not progress is being made over the course of time?

As educational researchers will tell you, if you want to assess someone's status, you have to specify what the definitions of good and bad are or, stated differently, what constitutes desirable and undesirable outcomes. Fortunately, when it comes to figuring out how we're doing spiritually, the Bible provides ample guidance in defining positive and negative outcomes.

For instance, to simplify matters, we might take three important passages of Scripture: (1) the Ten Commandments (see Exod. 20); (2) Jesus' Sermon on the Mount (see Matt. 5—7); and (3) the "fruit of the spirit" described by the apostle Paul (see Gal. 5). While these sections of the Bible do not contain everything that God hopes we will become, they provide a pretty robust guide to personal holiness. Study these passages and you will find that the following outcomes are identified as goals for our lives:

- Worship only God.
- Speak without profanity.
- Honor the Sabbath.
- Honor your parents.
- Avoid murdering people.
- Exhibit sexual purity.
- Honor people's possessions.
- Be truthful and honest.
- Be humble.
- Promote justice.
- Forgive people.
- Be a peacemaker.
- Be committed to Jesus.
- Avoid gossip.
- Celebrate and enjoy life.
- Love other people.
- Show kindness to all.
- Be generous with resources.
- Pray constantly.
- Be self-controlled.
- Be gentle.
- Refuse to be judgmental.
- Trust God and don't worry.
- Remain obedient to God.

If those are the outcomes that we seek to facilitate in our children's lives so that they become mature disciples of the Lord, then our assessments should reflect the presence or absence of those attributes. Further, if we want our assessments to be most helpful, we might incorporate degrees or levels of the presence or absence of those attributes.

Let's look at two examples (honor your parents and be self-controlled) to figure out what a helpful, albeit unprofessional, assessment of our children might look like. (This type of assessment can be carried out by parents or by a church's youth workers, but ideally it should be carried out by both.) We must then operationalize what these outcomes look like so that they can be measured.

In order to meaningfully operationalize these (or other) desired outcomes, we start by tying our search for clues (for spiritual growth) to the means of measurement. Here are some means through which we can evaluate outcomes:

- *Formal evaluation tools*—written tests, oral tests, essays, competitions and homework assignments

- *Self-report evaluation tools*—surveys, inventories and profiles

- *Conversation and dialogue*—language used, reasoning skills, foundational worldview expressed and interactive engagement

- *Observable behavior or perspectives*—attendance, volunteerism, invitations, donations, professed beliefs, memorized beliefs, physical condition and body language

- *Inferences from choices*—character of friends, media preferences, spending habits, social activism, attire and appearance

When we apply these means in the hope of gaining some insight into the young person's spiritual maturity, we look for specific bits of evidence. If we are seeking to find evidence that the child honors his or her parents, we might examine information available from the following:

- *Formal evaluation tools* (i.e., comments about parents in an essay or descriptions of parents in a homework assignment)

- *Children's reactions* to survey statements about parents and family as recorded in nonconfidential surveys

- *The language used* to describe children's relationships with their parents or exclamations about them (e.g., "oh, they always embarrass me")

- *Indicators of an underlying worldview* (i.e., the absence of a need to accept parental authority when it is not convenient or desirable to do so, as proposed in postmodernism)

- *Facial expressions and body language* when in the presence of parents and peers

- *The types of presents* (if any) given to parents on special occasions

- *Efforts to respect parents* through the choice of clothing worn to public events the parents attend with the child

> **PASTORAL** P **URGENT CONTENT** **ADVISORY**
>
> Do you begin to see that if we consciously seek clues to how our children are growing spiritually, then we will find more information than we may have otherwise believed exists?

The notion of being self-controlled, or self-governed, also can be measured in like manner. Information related to formal evaluation tools might be gained by determining if the child was able to complete the exam without cheating or complaining. Self-evaluation tools such as surveys could yield insights into how the young person intellectually and emotionally processed concepts and resources such as power and responsibility. Conversations with the youngster could indicate levels of moral and spiritual independence, or the willingness to disengage from inappropriate conversation with peers. Attendance at voluntary church events or service projects (i.e., no parental pressure attached) could tell something about the child's values and decision-making capacity. The appeal of certain peer groups and the child's inclination toward those groups might also reveal insight into his or her self-control.

Do you begin to see that if we consciously seek clues to how our children are growing spiritually, then we will find more information than we may have otherwise believed exists?

STILL LEERY?

Let me address two nagging concerns that may be bothering you at this point. The first is the feeling that creating and carrying out an evaluation process for your kids seems overwhelming. Chances are good that you have not engaged in any kind of focused effort to evaluate their spiritual growth, so you're starting from scratch in an endeavor that you are unfamiliar and uncomfortable with. Don't despair! Anytime you start something new, it may seem beyond your capabilities. How-ever, the best advice is to simply jump in and start someplace. Having some measures, even if they're incomplete or imperfect, is generally better than not having anything on which to base your judgments and plans. Select a handful of desirable spiritual outcomes, choose a couple of means of gathering information and see what you come up with. The more often you engage in such measurement, the more insightful your forays into the process will be—for you and the children you're examining. If you're like most adults who are new to this process, you'll also discover that the more you do it, the easier and more reliable it becomes.

The second concern has to do with recording what you discover. It might sound like overkill to try to keep track of the evaluation revelations, but over the course of time it will prove to be helpful. Remember that sometimes your memory misleads you, which can have unfortunate consequences for the children you are evaluating. Even more important is the fact that because most spiritual change is gradual in nature, when you are constantly working with those whom you wish to assess, a series of small improvements can easily be overlooked because of their incremental nature. (It's like the story of the frog in the kettle—when immersed in a pot of room temperature water, the amphibian will fail to notice the rise in the water temperature if the heat is increased slowly and consistently. Oblivious to the gradual change in surroundings, the frog will boil to death.) To be sure that you recognize changes and to respond intelligently, keep some record of the evaluation outcomes and how the children are changing over time.

How Do You Know for Sure?

Most believers refuse to assume that if someone calls him- or herself a Christian that he or she is truly saved; instead, they want to know for sure. That's the heart of one who knows Christ and wants to be sure He is known by all people, for the sake of the person and for Christ.

But why stop at knowing that a person is saved? Are we willing to allow "cheap grace" to prevail—that is, to allow people to accept God's offer of salvation but then never allow them to get beyond step one of the Christian life? Would you feel comfortable explaining to God that you were content to take people's statements about their spiritual life at face value and not even conducting a cursory evaluation of where they stood in order to help them advance in their development? Would you want other people to spiritually abandon you in that way?

Evaluation may seem rather businesslike, but consider this: God will evaluate how we lived, Jesus encouraged His followers to examine their hearts, and the Holy Spirit has been entrusted to us to enable us to live beyond the mundane. Where we choose to spend eternity, who we become and what we do matter to God. We owe it to Him to evaluate the lives of our children so that they may have and exploit every opportunity to become pleasing servants of the living God.

CHAPTER 8

IT'S TIME
TO PRODUCE
SOME SPIRITUAL
CHAMPIONS

Children often need reassurances that they are loved by those whom they trust and depend upon. My oldest daughter loves to ask challenging questions of her mother and me. Several years ago, while spending a laid-back Saturday lounging around the house, she wandered into my study where I was working at the computer.

"Daddy," she began innocently, "do you love me?"

GEORGE BARNA

After turning away from the computer to give her my full attention, I affirmed that she was more important to me than anything else in the world and that I loved her very dearly. She smiled and then let loose the big one.

"How do I know you really love me?"

Ah, the thoughts that went racing through my mind. *Let's see. I wiped your poopy behind every day for two years, ran a car into the ground carting you to sports practices, spent hours awake late at night holding you or calming you when you had earaches or stomachaches, spent more money than I'd care to tally on special adventures and events, played silly games until I couldn't bear it any longer, and so on.*

"I hug you and kiss you and tell you all the time how much I love you," I replied.

"Yeah, but how do I know you really mean it?" she pressed forward, digging for the golden nugget of truth.

"I work really hard to make the money that provides your food, clothing, home and toys."

"Yeah, but you have to do that. That's what every parent has to do, but that doesn't mean you love me."

I invited her to sit on my lap while I told her the ultimate, indisputable way that she could know that I loved her more than anything else on the planet. "Buddy, I do everything I can to try to raise you up to be the woman that God made you and wants you to be. There is nothing more important than that you love, obey and serve God with all your heart, mind, strength and soul. And I do everything I can to help you be a little girl who grows up to be a big girl who is God's pleasing and faithful servant. There's nothing more special that any parent can do than to help his or her child honor God; and I will never stop trying to do the things that bring you closer to Him. That's more important than buying you nice clothes or giving you a cell phone, than letting you see every movie you want to see or giving you the biggest room in the house. I really want God and other people throughout the world to be blessed by who you are."

> **PASTORAL P URGENT CONTENT ADVISORY**
>
> The transformation of children into spiritual champions may not happen even if we devote our best resources to the task, but the possibility is worth the risk.

Her big, dark eyes continued to stare intently into mine for a few seconds after I finished delivering my best shot. Then she pursed her lips, grinned, nodded her head up and down a few times, and simply said, "Okay," and went bounding out of the room. She has never asked me that question again. I hope it is because she sensed the truthfulness and sincerity of my reply.

A SHARED GOAL

Each of us who has the privilege of relating to young children these days shares a special goal: to help transform those children into spiritual champions. It will not happen by accident. It may not happen even if we devote our best resources to that task, but the possibility is worth the risk. In fact, this isn't really a risk at all since our personal success in life is completely wrapped up in our willingness to nurture these young people.

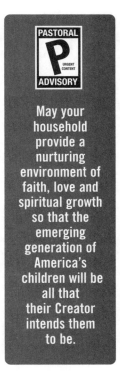

If you have not yet reached the point of embarrassment over the fact that most adults—perhaps even you—abdicate your children's moral and spiritual development to illegitimate usurpers of that responsibility (e.g., schools, the media, legislatures, judges and even churches), then I pray that the Holy Spirit will heighten your sensitivity to this travesty with all due haste. We have no right to complain about how our children develop if we are not heavily and purposefully investing in those outcomes. Those who fill the gap in our absence are mere substitutes for us when we don't pull our weight. If we default on our responsibility, we cannot blame those substitutes for making the most of the opportunity. This is, after all, part of the battle for the minds and hearts of humanity.

May your household provide a nurturing environment of faith, love and spiritual growth so that the emerging generation of America's children will be all that their Creator intends them to be.

I pray that in the years to come you will seize the opportunities that God provides to you, as a committed disciple of Jesus Christ, to enable your home and those of other believers to be places of victory in the turbulent and relentless spiritual battle for those young hearts, minds and souls. May your household provide a nurturing environment of faith, love and spiritual growth so that the emerging generation of America's children will be all that their creator intends them to be.

ENDNOTES

Chapter 1: The State of American Children

1. Source unknown.
2. For reasons that will be explained as we progress, it is during these ages that people are experiencing the formation of their characters and souls. While people are always changing and God can impact a person's life at any age, an abundance of research has shown how malleable young people are during these early years—more so than at any other time of their lives.
3. U.S. Bureau of the Census, "Facts for Features: Back to School," *Census Bureau Home Page*, August 2002. http://www.census.gov (accessed September 5, 2003).
4. Ibid.
5. Children's Defense Fund, *The State of Children in America's Union: A 2002 Action Guide to Leave No Child Behind, May 2002* (Washington, DC: n.p., 2002), p. 13.
6. *Business Week* (March 19, 2001), p. 68.
7. An article in *USA Today* (June 11, 2001), p. 1, described a study by the National Institutes of Health that showed more than 75 percent of high school dropouts have reading difficulties, and 50 percent of all adolescents and teens who have a criminal record have reading problems.
8. Children's Defense Fund, *The State of Children in America's Union*, n.p.
9. Jeffrey M. Jones, "Little Change in the Way Americans Grade K-12 Schools: Continue to Give Higher Grades to Local Schools Than to Schools Nationwide," *The Gallup Organization*. http://www.gallup.com/poll/releases/pr030827.asp (accessed September 10, 2003).
10. This perspective is verified by surveys reported by the U.S. Bureau of the Census website, http://www.census.gov (accessed September 9, 2001), which show only one-third of parents identify safety issues, three-tenths list social pressures and one-quarter note social pressures regarding body image as being present at their child's school. Most of the parents interviewed felt there is more pressure on their child to perform well academically than to not perform well.
11. Children's Defense Fund, *The State of Children in America's Union*, n.p.
12. "Pastor's Weekly Briefing," *Focus on the Family* (October 11, 2002), p. 1.
13. Centers for Disease Control and Prevention, *STD Surveillance Report, 1998* (Washington, DC), pp. 49-54.
14. Pamela Lam-Yip, "Youth Violence in the United States and Texas," *Legislative Council* (May 2000), pp. 2-7.
15. Source unknown.
16. Alexandra Marks, "More Teens Have Sex and Fewer Parents Know," *Pastors.com*, July 2, 2003. http://www.pastors.com/article.asp?ArtID=4346 (accessed September 5, 2003).
17. Naomi Lopez, "The State of Children: What Parents Should Know About Government's Efforts to Assist Children," *Pacific Research Organization*, August 1998. http://www.pacificresearch.org/pub/sab/health/state_of_children/children.html# summary (accessed September 5, 2003).

18. "Selected Key Indicators of Child Well-Being," *The Annie E. Casey Foundation*, 1990-2000. http://www.aecf.org (accessed July 1, 2003).

19. U.S. Bureau of the Census, *Census Bureau Home Page*, March 30, 2001. http://www.census.gov (accessed September 5, 2003).

20. EPM Communications, *Research Alert Yearbook, 2003* (New York: n.p., n.d.), pp. 97-102.

21. These figures are drawn from a survey conducted in 2001 by WGBH and Applied Research and Consulting and from the annual tracking study, *Monitoring the Future*, produced by the Institute of Social Research at the University of Michigan.

22. Henry J. Kaiser Family Foundation, *Kids and Media, November 1999* (Menlo Park, CA: n.p., n.d.), n.p.

23. EPM Communications, *Research Alert Yearbook, 2003*, (New York: n.p., n.d.) pp. 97-102, 317-326.

24. Ibid.

25. Ibid.

26. Ibid.

27. Ibid.

28. The Gallup Organization, "The Gallup Tuesday Briefing," *The Gallup Organization*, May 15, 2001. http://www.gallup.com (accessed August 2003).

Chapter 2: The Spiritual Health of Our Children

1. His intention to hold us accountable is clearly expressed in Ecclesiastes 11:9 and Romans 14:12. A wealth of other passages such as Matthew 12:36, Exodus 32:34, Psalm 10:13, Ezekiel 7:3 and Hosea 8:13 support such judgment.

2. Understanding our purpose and the meaning of life emerges from the foundation of our considerations, which is known as a worldview. For a more comprehensive explanation of common worldviews, their development and their implications, see George Barna, *Think Like Jesus* (Nashville, TN: Integrity Publishers, 2003); Charles Colson and Nancy Pearcey, *How Now Shall We Live* (Wheaton, IL: Tyndale House Publishers, 2001); and David Naugle, *Worldview* (Grand Rapids, MI: Eerdmans Publishing, 2002).

3. By "postmodern," I am referring to the widespread philosophy that says there are no moral absolutes, one's views should not be imposed upon anyone else, you must be tolerant and accepting of all other viewpoints because there is no all-encompassing right moral or spiritual position, and each individual is his or her own moral standard. For a more expansive understanding of this vacuous worldview, see George Barna, *Think Like Jesus* (Nashville, TN: Integrity Publishers, 2003); Gene Edward Veith, *Postmodern Times* (Wheaton, IL: Crossway Books, 1994); and James Sire, *The Universe Next Door* (Downers Grove, IL: InterVarsity Press, 1997).

4. Jack Hayford, *Blessing Your Children* (Ventura, CA: Regal Books, 2002), p. 136.

5. In our research, we do not categorize people as "born again" based on their using that label to describe themselves. We categorize people based upon their beliefs, not their self-description, church affiliation or religious practices. The statistics cited in this section are based on nationwide research among a random sample of 907 teenagers, of which 154 were 13 years old.

6. As in the born-again population, when we classify someone as an evangelical, it is not based on self-description, church affiliation or religious practices; instead, it is based

solely upon their beliefs as described in this paragraph. The 5 percent who are classified as evangelicals represent about one-eighth of the born-again category of which they are a part.

Chapter 4: What Kids Need

1. The influence agents in each of the three tiers are not listed in order of influence, because we are not able to determine, at this time, what that sequence is. At this stage, we are working with both qualitative and quantitative data but do not have sufficient confidence in the reliability of the statistical measures used to posit any definitive ranking of the elements.
2. Apart from our research, studies by individuals and institutions such as Harvard psychiatrist Robert Coles, The Search Institute and Columbia University have indicated similar findings.
3. For more information on a biblical worldview and the development process, see George Barna, *Think Like Jesus* (Nashville, TN: Integrity Publishers, 2003).
4. God has a unique and compelling vision for every person who relates to Him through the grace received by the death and resurrection of Jesus Christ. Vision, which is a compelling mental portrait of a preferable future that God conveys to His followers for the purpose of advancing the Kingdom, becomes the defining characteristic of a true Christian. It is the means by which the person puts his or her faith in Christ into action. For a more extensive discussion of this practice, see George Barna, *Turning Vision into Action* (Ventura, CA: Regal Books, 1996).
5. See George Barna, *Think Like Jesus* (Nashville, TN: Integrity Publishers, 2003).

Chapter 6: How Churches Help to Raise Spiritual Champions

1. A taped presentation of this information by George Barna, entitled *Transforming Children into Spiritual Champions*, is available in video or DVD form. The video can be acquired from Barna Research at http://www.barna.org. A DVD containing the presentation can be purchased from Gospel Light at http://www.gospellight.com.
2. For a more complete description of leadership, the four different aptitudes that leaders possess and how great team-based leadership works, read about the research Barna Research Group conducted on this topic in George Barna, *The Power of Team Leadership* (Colorado Springs, CO: WaterBrook Press, 2001). When this approach to leadership is utilized, the entire Church and community benefit; and leaders experience a higher level of satisfaction, impact and joy in their leading.

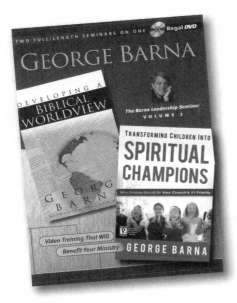
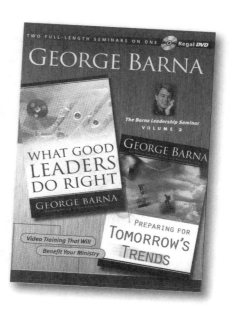

ALSO AVAILABLE FROM
GEORGE BARNA

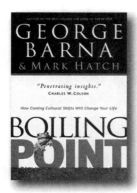

Boiling Point
ISBN 0-8307-3305-1
ISBN 978-0-8307-3305-7

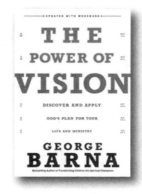

The Power of Vision
ISBN 0-8307-4728-1
ISBN 978-0-8307-4728-3

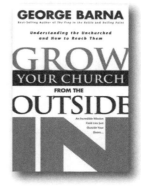

**Grow Your Church
from the Outside In**
ISBN 0-8307-3075-3
ISBN 978-0-8307-3075-9

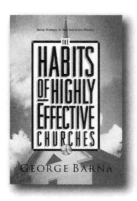

**The Habits of Highly
Effective Churches**
ISBN 0-8307-1860-5
ISBN 978-0-8307-1860-3

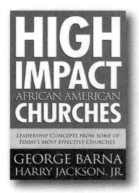

**High Impact African-
American Churches**
ISBN 0-8307-3898-3
ISBN 978-0-8307-3898-4

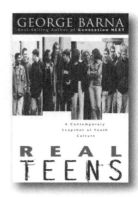

Real Teens
ISBN 0-8307-2663-2
ISBN 978-08307-2663-9